Popular Day Hikes 4

Vancouver Island

Theo Dombrowski

RMB

Rocky Mountain Books
www.rmbooks.com

Library and Archives Canada Cataloguing in Publication

Dombrowski, Theo, 1947-, author
    Vancouver Island / Theo Dombrowski.

(Popular day hikes ; 4)
Includes bibliographical references and index.
Issued in print and electronic formats.
ISBN 978-1-77160-007-1 (pbk.).—ISBN 978-1-77160-008-8 (html).—
ISBN 978-1-77160-009-5 (pdf)

    1. Hiking—British Columbia—Vancouver Island—Guidebooks.
2. Trails—British Columbia—Vancouver Island—Guidebooks.
3. Vancouver Island (B.C.)—Guidebooks. I. Title. II. Series: Popular day hikes ; 4

GV199.44.C22V35 2014b   796.5109711'2   C2013-908269-7
                                        C2013-908270-0

Front cover photo: Fast mountain stream in Vancouver Island, Canada © Yevgen Timashov
Title page: A typical section of forest along the northern part of the route. Gigantic old trees are interspersed with younger growth, moss, salmon berries, rotting logs, and sword ferns. (2)
Back cover photo: from Hike 6. Gowlland Tod Park Jocelyn Peak Loop

Printed in Canada

Rocky Mountain Books acknowledges the financial support for its publishing program from the Government of Canada through the Canada Book Fund (CBF) and the Canada Council for the Arts, and from the province of British Columbia through the British Columbia Arts Council and the Book Publishing Tax Credit.

This book was produced using FSC®-certified, acid-free paper, processed chlorine free and printed with vegetable-based inks.

Disclaimer

The actions described in this book may be considered inherently dangerous activities. Individuals undertake these activities at their own risk. The information put forth in this guide has been collected from a variety of sources and is not guaranteed to be completely accurate or reliable. Many conditions and some information may change owing to weather and numerous other factors beyond the control of the authors and publishers. Individual climbers and/or hikers must determine the risks, use their own judgment, and take full responsibility for their actions. Do not depend on any information found in this book for your own personal safety. Your safety depends on your own good judgment based on your skills, education and experience.

    It is up to the users of this guidebook to acquire the necessary skills for safe experiences and to exercise caution in potentially hazardous areas. The authors and publishers of this guide accept no responsibility for your actions or the results that occur from another's actions, choices or judgments. If you have any doubt as to your safety or your ability to attempt anything described in this guidebook, do not attempt it.

Introduction

Vancouver Island is blessed with huge numbers of beautiful routes and trails to and amongst unforgettable peaks, along clear, rushing rivers and around picturesque lakes. Unfortunately, it is less well endowed, thus far at least, with good trails long enough to be considered "day hikes" and yet easily accessible on dependable roads. The hikes selected for this book are amongst the comparatively few that meet those criteria. Many beautiful routes have been excluded because they are accessible only unreliably, along logging roads subject to washouts and closures. Others were omitted because they are undeveloped routes where first-time visitors could easily lose their way. Still others make gorgeous walks but are too short to make much of a day hike. This is especially true in the northern part of Vancouver Island, where short walks, long coastal trails and faint routes account for nearly all of the walks.

A lot of great hiking is suited only to multi-day backpackers, particularly along the ridges of Strathcona Provincial Park. The same is true for the multi-day oceanfront trails for which Vancouver Island is world famous.

These oceanfront trails are excluded for another reason. This book is dedicated to the mountains, lakes and rivers and the wealth of wilderness experiences they provide. Those who would love to enjoy Vancouver Island's hugely varied coastline should turn to the companion volume, *Seaside Walks on Vancouver Island*.

Within this group of inland trails, visitors will find great variety. Some are wide, easy paths with little change in elevation and suitable for the whole family. At the other extreme are strenuous treks up some of the island's highest mountains.

Almost all of these trails, though, are "popular." This is particularly the case where they are maintained by municipalities, regional districts or provincial or national parks. Some are made accessible by public-spirited logging companies. Also included here are a few wonderful trails that are part of no system as yet but are made by volunteers and enthusiasts. Some of them, quite new, are popular chiefly with locals and eager walking groups so far – but as word spreads, these are becoming increasingly favoured by the general public. Thus, a few of the hikes in this volume do not have clearly signposted trailheads. The trails themselves, however, are almost invariably smooth sailing.

Weather

Vancouver Island's climate is, of course, West Coast Marine, and that means moderate temperatures and considerable moisture. Be aware, though, that both of these general qualities have many exceptions. Although elevations are low compared to, say, the Rockies, the mountains of Vancouver Island are, like their larger cousins, subject to sudden changes and extreme weather. Always be prepared for a downpour or, except in July and August, the possibility of a freak snowstorm. Lightning storms are extremely rare at any time of year.

The valleys and coastal areas, in contrast, are fairly reliably moderate most of the year, though again subject to unpredictable rain. One of the glories of hiking the trails described in this book, therefore, is that many of them can be enjoyed all year round – at least on good days. Even many of the mountains, those with low avalanche danger, are regularly climbed in snowy conditions. Only hikers with the proper experience and equipment, however, should venture into the mountains in winter.

Wildlife encounters

Vancouver Island does not have grizzlies. While it does have black bears – and many of them – they seem, mysteriously, even less likely to be aggressive than their mainland kin. There have been a few exceptions, however. Hikers should make their presence noisily known and avoid confrontations. Bear bells, noisemakers (some recommend a compressed-air horn over "bangers"), and pepper spray increase the safety margin for small groups in remote areas and in high-incidence locations such as berry fields and salmon-filled rivers in the fall.

Walkers with children will be wise to keep them close by. Cougar attacks on children, though rare, are more common on Vancouver Island than anywhere else in Canada.

Wolves and elk, a concern in some places, are so elusive as to be not worth worrying about (except around Cape Scott, where they have recently become a problem). Vancouver Island has no porcupines, coyotes, foxes, skunks, moose, wolverines or any other potentially problematic animals.

Drinking water

Though locals traditionally have drunk water from fast-rushing mountain streams, for day hikes there is no need to risk infection or even carry water purification chemicals or filters. It is best to bring domestic water. For strenuous hikes, it is best to use a bladder and drinking tube to allow steady rehydration.

Safety

- The biggest danger on remote and difficult trails is probably a twisted ankle in combination with hypothermia. Walking poles, good boots, a first aid kit and proper clothing – always erring on the side of prudence – are sensible precautions. Cell phones work on most mountain tops and a few remote coastal areas.
- Avoid taking short cuts, especially in mountains. The likelihood is that you will encounter dangerous terrain.

- In remote areas, the ideal group size is three or more. On easy, busy trails, your judgment can obviously come into play.
- Always be prepared to turn back if weather, fitness or morale become issues.
- In the unlikely event of a lightning storm, avoid high, exposed land.
- If there is low cloud or fog, avoid climbing to the tops of mountains, where the distance between marker cairns can be fairly large. A GPS or compass (and knowing how to use them!) in combination with a good map can increase safety enormously. Several island mountains have ridges that converge toward the peak. While going up in low visibility may be easy and obvious, finding the right ridge on the way down in those conditions may not be.
- It is difficult to predict when snow will be gone from a particular route; conditions vary enormously from year to year. Lingering snow patches can often make a climb easier and the descent good fun. This is the case with almost all of the hikes in the book. However, in some instances, they can make finding a trail difficult and, worse, cause a dangerously uncontrolled slide.

Clothing and equipment

Much depends on the location of the trail, the time of year and the weather forecast for a particular day. As a general rule, it is better to take along too many clothing options rather than too few. A rain jacket may add half a kilo to your pack but it could prove invaluable. Quick-dry materials are ideal; avoid cotton, including jeans. Insects, at altitude, can sometimes be a problem, so bring repellent and, even in hot weather, long pants (or zip-offs). Trail runners or "approach shoes" are fine for easy trails, but full boots with ankle support and good grip can vastly improve your experience. Soft hiking boots are good enough for every route in this book

– and less likely than stiff boots to produce blisters. For large snow patches, gaiters can be helpful. Sunglasses are necessary and walking poles are often a real asset.

Numbered text

For clarity and ease of reference, the trail descriptions are written in short, numbered paragraphs. Some photo captions also contain numbers, which refer to the correspondingly numbered paragraphs in the text.

Optional side routes

Options to the main routes are set in blue type following the main descriptions.

Difficulty

These sections describe, not the exertion required on a particular route, but the nature of the terrain and any need for caution because of loose rock, roots, mud, lingering snow, slippery boardwalks and so on. While you may have to cross small streams, you will be able to use bridges over significant streams for all trails included in this book. Almost all log bridges have at least one handrail and a good walking surface.

For those not familiar with the term, "scrambling," as used in some of the descriptions, refers to crossing areas, usually of solid rock, that are steep and irregular enough that some use of hands is necessary. Normally, though, scrambling, involves nothing more than being somewhat careful and a little nimble.

Distance, height gain and duration of hikes

Distances may be given as out and back or as loops. Distance figures can be misleading, however. A 5 km hike on a steep, rough trail can seem many, many times longer than 5 km on an easy trail. Even calculating distances can be difficult, since lots of little knolls and twists can lead, in effect, to what actually is a longer trail than the distance number alone would suggest. When looking at the quoted length in planning your hike, be sure to consider the height gain and trail difficulty information as well.

Height gain is the net difference between a route's high and low points. But in fact, some trails have many small ascents and descents which, in effect, make for a more strenuous hike than the height gain figure by itself might suggest.

Of course, it is the combination of distance, height gain and personal speed that determines the overall length of a hike. "Naismith's Rule" will help you plan: allow 1 hour for every 5 km and add 1 hour for every 600 m you ascend. Most people need an additional 25 to 50 per cent. After two or three trips you will learn to adjust for your own personal speed. The durations that result are ascent times. Descents are usually faster, but if the terrain is steep and the footing uncertain, descending can actually be slower than ascending.

Season

As already noted, most of these trails are hiked all year round, but in winter, mountains are tackled only by those with experience and proper equipment. The lower the elevation, of course, the less likely it is that you will encounter snow in winter. Even a 400 m hill, though, may have snow at the top when there is none at sea level. Winter and spring tend to be the muddiest times of year. Even in a rainy autumn, mud can be slow to develop. Conversely, even in a dry spring, mud can be slow to dry up.

Sketch maps

Red lines indicate main trails. Red dashed lines are options. Black dashed lines are other trails and generally are shown only where they intersect with routes being described.

Area Map

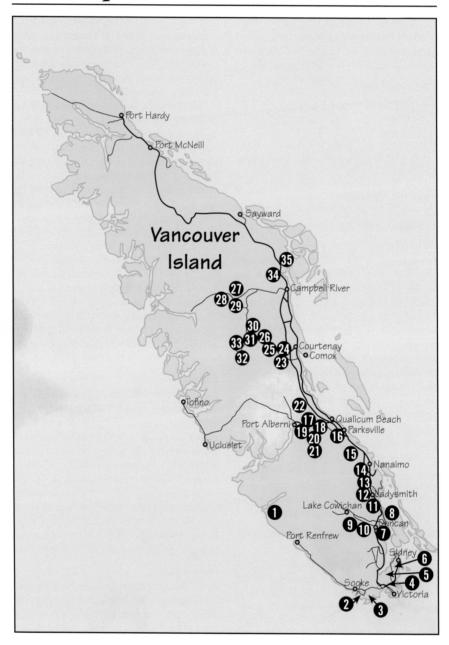

The Hikes

Meadows dotted with Garry oak partway up the steep section from Hike 5 Mount Finlayson

1. Carmanah Walbran

7.4 km return
Start height: 220 m
Streambed: 140 m
Easy
All season (except when too wet)

Iconic old-growth giants in one of the best examples of temperate-zone rainforest on Vancouver Island. Many claim a "mystic" presence amongst the ancient trees in this isolated wilderness valley. Winding paths with boardwalks and viewing platforms next to a small river.

Start: From Highway 1 north of Duncan, take the signposted turn for Carmanah Walbran toward Cowichan Lake. When you reach Cowichan Lake, follow the South Shore Road until you get to Nitinat Main, a logging road. When you come to the signposted turn to Junction South, turn left onto South Main. Cross the Caycuse River bridge, turn right and follow Rossander Main. The road, 29 km long, becomes increasingly rough and crowded with small alders. Signs mark the way well, but returning can be a bit of a trick unless you keep a sharp eye out for small signs, one of them spray painted onto a rock.

Difficulty: Currently many of the board-walks are usable but breaking down. In spring there may be the occasional fallen tree. Very slippery when wet (which is much of the time), the ramps and walkways have mesh, but a lot of it is currently broken or patchy. In wet weather there are a few muddy patches. If and when more of the original trail is reopened, the whole walk will be more challenging.

1. The first section of the trail is an old roadbed, sloping gradually toward a junction. The left branch leads to a camping area, while the path to the valley and the main trail for this hike forks right.

2. The descending trail is generally broad, evenly graded gravel, winding to the valley bottom. Amid mostly hemlock and cedar, the path passes one side route and a viewing platform for one of the largest trees, the "Coast Tower" (once 91 m tall, but now having a broken top).

3. At the T-junction, turn left onto the "Valley Mist Trail." In the valley bottom, most of the huge trees are Sitka spruce. One of these, the world's largest at 95 m tall, located farther down the valley, is no longer open to the public, but many other awe-inspiring giants grow along the open section of trail. The trail is generally level, though rising and dropping over some knolls. The first featured and signposted tree is the "Hollow Tree" a short distance along. Thereafter the trail dips close to the creek for a view of the amazingly clear water running over white river rocks. The first section of trail ends at a cluster of three large spruce signposted as "The Three Sisters" (79 m tall). There is also a camping area here. In fact, it is worth-while leaving the main trail to make your way onto the gravel bars of the creek so you can stand back and get a sense of the whole forest and its surroundings.

4. Return to the T-junction and head down the southern section. The first part of this segment has a different character from the northern part of the trail. It climbs a little up staircases to run along a ridge around a bend in the creek and generally stays close to the creek. In spring look for pink fawn lilies and trilliums. Take the signposted side trail to the "Heaven Tree." Two features make this enormous tree distinctive. First, it is approached from a small clearing so you can fully appreciate its size. Second, it has a split trunk and therefore a magnificent base, even sprouting licorice ferns. The trail ends at

"Heaven Grove," with one giant tree identified for its amazing height, 81 m. Here too, you will see informative signs about the Randy Stoltman Commemorative Grove. The tallest tree here towers 89 m.

5. Return to the trailhead, lingering at some of the best viewing spots en route.

Option:

Beyond Three Sisters, the trail is not maintained and a sign warns "Trail Closed Ahead." Going farther is not forbidden, though. So if you are feeling adventurous, you may wish to extend your walk.

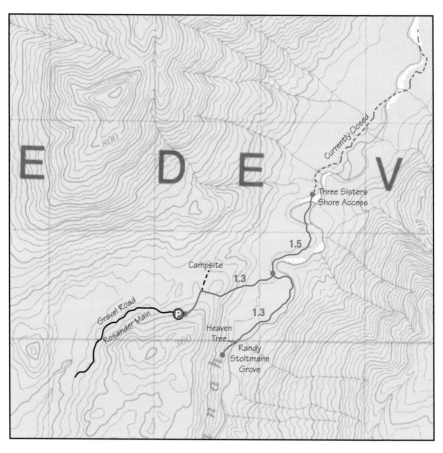

The startlingly clear water of Carmanah Creek with glimpses of
the mountainside of the Carmanah Valley (3)

The southern branch of the trail begins with several sequences of stairs among some particularly striking tree forms (4)

2. Mount Maguire

8.5 km loop
Start height: 54 m (drops to sea
   level)
High point: 268 m
Height gain: 270 m
Moderate
All year

*Lots of variety – shady patches
amongst large old firs and cedars,
sunny bluffs with arbutus and moss,
rocky coastline and high views
over the Strait of Juan de Fuca
toward the Olympic Peninsula.*

Start: From Highway 1 about 8 km
northwest of Victoria, take exit 10 toward
Colwood. Drive 3.5 km south along Old
Island Highway, and at the traffic lights
at Goldstream Road go straight through
to begin Sooke Road. After 16 km turn
left onto Gillespie Road for 5.6 km. Turn
right onto East Sooke Road for 8 km, then
left onto Pike Road and follow it until you
see the large sign and parking lot for
Iron Mine Bay.

Difficulty: Much of the route follows old
roadbeds that have a history associated
with mining and logging. Two comparatively short sections – one along the
coast, the other to the summit of the
small mountain – involve much rougher
trail and some care with footing. Expect
muddy sections on Anderson Cove
Trail and Coppermine Trail in the wetter
months.

1. Walk past the washrooms and information signs along a wide, smooth track
toward the distant ocean. You will pass
some large mature trees as well as some
interesting old stumps that still have the
grooves once used by tree fallers to place
boards to stand on.

2. Take the first trail on the left, signposted for Mt. Maguire and Anderson Cove
Trail. You will cross a small bridge and in a
short distance see another sign indicating
the Coast Trail and Iron Mine Trail. This
will be your return route. Carry straight on
past these signs along a generally direct,
smooth path, often wet in some sections.
At some points, salmonberry and salal can

crowd the way.

3. The trail narrows and begins to climb
over increasingly rocky and irregular
bluffs. As you traverse upward along the
south slope of the Maguire ridge you will
pass several open, grassy bluffs dropping
steeply into the forest. When the trail
switchbacks sharply downward into a
shady cleft you will quickly come to the
signposted summit route. Turn left. The
trail ascends fairly steeply over natural
rock steps but requires no scrambling.
When you come to a small side trail
to the right, go the short distance to a
good viewpoint, then return to the main
route. You will find the path spiralling
counterclockwise through small pines
to approach the summit viewpoint and
bench from the north.

4. Return the way you came along
the summit track, dropping down to
Anderson Cove Trail. Turn left and follow
this a short distance to Coppermine Trail.
Turn right and begin a fairly consistent,
broad descent toward the coast. You will
see a sign for the narrow Anderson Cove
and Swamp Bypass on your left. This trail
is prettier than the wide road but joins the
road after a short distance. A little later on,
an interpretive sign gives you information
about the old mine shaft entrance visible
from the trail. You will see a broken rock
slope on your right, and if you're interested you can have a look at two cave-like
mine shafts.

5. Running generally downhill on low
ground between a low crest on either side,

the trail eventually comes to a junction. Take the right fork (though noting that the left fork allows a slightly longer variation, described below as Option 1).

6. You will join the signposted Coast Trail, which is not on the coast itself but in a bushy gully. Taking the right fork, you will soon emerge from the gully onto the open coast. This end of the Coast Trail is comparatively rough, requiring some careful footing over roots, up and down rocky outcroppings and past some cliff edges.

7. Shortly before coming to Iron Mine Bay, take the Mt. Maguire trail signposted on your right. The trail begins by climbing over mossy knolls and through sprinkled trees before levelling a little and entering deeper forests (where, in April, you may spot some lady's slippers). For 1 km the

trail first winds upward through a trough between ridges, then climbs onto the west ridge before running along its crest and dropping down to a bit of table land. The descent to a T-junction is comparatively steep.

8. Counterintuitively, turn left at this junction (signposted to the right for Mt. Maguire and Anderson Cove) to join with the main Iron Mine Bay/Pike Road trail in a little over 100 m. Turn right to return to your vehicle.

Options:

East Sooke is a maze of interconnecting trails. Most of these are well signposted and clearly marked. Be warned, though, that without a good map of the park you can become disoriented in spite of the signs. In addition, the Coast Trail has many user-made side routes that lead to dead ends

The viewpoint from the top, with the Olympic Peninsula across the Strait of Juan de Fuca (3)

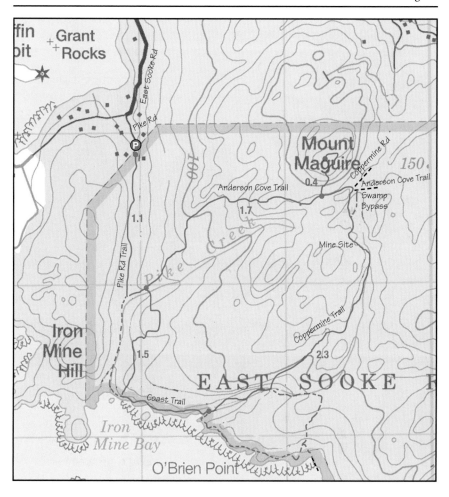

at steep sections. Always make sure you are following the trail indicated with orange tags. The two most obvious choices for those hiking to Mt. Maguire are one slightly longer option and one slightly shorter one.

1. For the longer option, at the sign described in step 5 above, turn left instead of right. This will take you back away from the coast and uphill for some distance before dropping directly toward the shore at the head of a gully. Turn right to follow a rugged but beautiful section of coastline

before joining the route described above. This option adds about 1.5 km to the overall distance.

2. For a slightly shorter option, walk the Coast Trail all the way to Iron Mine Bay. A broad, straight roadbed leads directly from the shore to the parking lot. This shortcut only saves about 500 m, but it avoids a lot of climbing over comparatively rough trail. Be aware, though, that this route omits some lovely areas of sunny bluffs and shady gullies of big trees.

Nearing the northwest end of the coast trail, with Secretary Island just visible (6)

One of the abandoned mine shafts just off Coppermine Road (4)

3. Matheson Lake to Roche Cove

7.2 km loop
Start height: 62 m
High point: 180 m
Height gain: insignificant, but several
  short ups and downs
Easy
All season (a detour of one section
  is necessary in winter)

A varied sequence of trails past good swimming and views of a wilderness lake surrounded by some old-growth forest. The whole loop includes a high view of the lake, deep forest, an ocean cove and a creekside trail.

Start: From Highway 1 westbound from Victoria, take the Colwood exit. Follow the Old Island Highway, which turns into Sooke Road. From Sooke Road, turn left on Happy Valley Road, then right on Rocky Point Road, and right again on Matheson Lake Park Road, which leads to the park entrance. Allow approximately 35 minutes driving time from Victoria.

Difficulty: With little altitude change and generally broad, easy trails, there are few difficulties. Some of the trails have roots and rocks where care should be taken not to twist an ankle. Some of the trails can be muddy in winter and early spring.

1. Walk past the outhouses and along the wide, smooth path sloping toward the lake. Instead of turning down to the beach, keep straight to follow the trail that runs parallel to the shore, first past some low, rocky bluffs (used by swimmers and fishers), then round a promontory with good views of a small island. The trail swings back, partly on boardwalks, to leave the lakeshore and avoid a swampy area.

2. As the trail rejoins the lake, look for a small, user-made trail leading straight up the slope through salal and firs to the Galloping Goose, a rails-to-trails route. (If you miss the little connecting path, keep on the park trail until it joins the Goose about 500 m farther along, and then turn right to point 3).

3. Leave the Galloping Goose on a small, user-made path past a huge fir full of woodpecker holes. Follow this track as it crosses a tiny stream and climbs to the top of an open bluff. Leave the through trail for superb views onto Matheson Lake.

4. Rejoin the trail as it descends into a forest with waist-high ferns and comes to a T-junction with a broader path. This route, called Cedar Grove Trail, is mostly an old roadbed that is shared with horses. Turning left takes you a short distance back to the Galloping Goose. For the full loop described here, turn right and follow the wide, even trail to a signposted junction. Turn sharp left.

5. After a short distance, turn right to rejoin the Galloping Goose. If you are getting tired, you can shortcut by turning left instead of right and rejoining the Goose at the east tip of Roche Cove rather than the west end. (Note that you are only 300 m from a parking lot with washrooms.) Once on the Galloping Goose, you can catch glimpses of Roche Cove, this curious inland reach of the ocean many kilometres away from the open straits. Turn left along the Goose and walk until you see a signposted trail on your right leading you down to Roche Cove and Matheson Creek.

6. After taking a look at the cove, retrace your route a few steps to join the creekside trail back to the western tip of Matheson Lake and another signposted junction. If this track is muddy and/or closed (as it is in winter), you can return to the Galloping Goose and turn right to reach Matheson Lake.

7. Turn right at a signposted trailhead to follow the south shore of Matheson Lake. The trail on this side is generally rougher than the one on the north side, requiring some climbing and descending over rocky sections. Though the route is often away from the lakeshore, several side branches lead to view spots. The circuit trail brings you back to the parking lot.

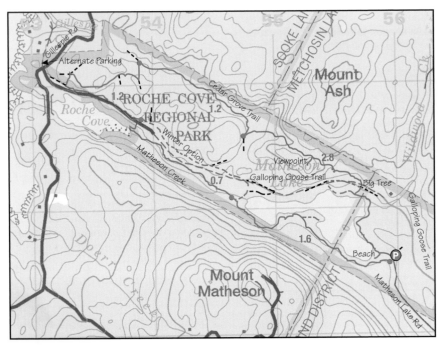

Sea blush, stone crop and many other flowers are common on the rocky outcroppings along of the Galloping Goose (5)

The beach at the south end of the lake and close to the parking lot is a popular swimming spot (1)

Tiny Matheson Creek flows from the lake into Roche Cove (6)

4. Thetis Lake

10 km loop (many other options)
High point: 131 m
Height gain: 80 m to Seymour Hill,
   many small ups and down along
   whole route
Easy
All season

A sequence of linked trails provides a cross-section of ecosystem diversity: oak and arbutus meadows, cedar and fern streams, lakes and bluffs, busy lakeside trails and remote, little-used paths.

Start: From downtown Victoria, drive north on Douglas Street as it becomes Highway 1. Some 7 km from the centre of town take exit 10 to View Royal and Colwood. Then, 1.5 km later, having merged onto Highway 1A, the Old Island Highway, turn right at the Shell station onto Six Mile Road. Drive straight ahead under Highway 1 to arrive at Thetis Lake Park.

Difficulty: Most of the trails are well used and clearly signposted, though the older colour-coded system, sometimes useful, is currently a little chaotic. Some of the trails on this suggested route loop off from the most-used circuit trail. These can be fairly narrow and in a few places quite muddy well into May. Always, the major difficulty is finding your way forward. Not only is there a huge maze of official trails winding through the knolls and woods, but also there are at least as many user-made, unofficial trails criss-crossing one another.

1. From the parking lot, pass the signposted map and take a right fork down a trail with a blue sign reading "Lewis Clark Trail." Gradually head up Seymour Hill through scattered oaks and firs. In spring you will pass stunning arrays of wildflowers, with fawn lilies, shooting stars, ocean spray and camas prominent. Ignore trails to the right to walk past a small, dammed pond. Take a right fork (red mark on a tree) and circle to the left, ignoring right forks. Ascend past increasingly open knolls to reach the broad and uneven summit of Seymour Hill. You will probably want to

leave the main route to explore some side trails on the summit for views over Thetis Lake and toward the forested hills to the northwest.

2. Carry on along the ridge, gradually descending along the largest track while ignoring two small side paths to the left. Next ignore two small trails to the right. When you reach a distinct T-junction, with the ridge above you on the left and a wooded gully below, turn right onto a large trail heading more downhill.

3. Two minutes later you will come to another T-junction. Again take the right fork to head downhill. The trail traverses through small meadows and increasingly dense trees. A bit of blue paint on a large fir will confirm you are on the route. When the trail levels out, the densely growing salal crowds in. You may glimpse a reedy marsh (shown on maps as a pond) through the trees to your right. The trail can be muddy just before a T-junction with a very broad trail. Turn right and go a short way to Highlands Road. You will see a sign for Trillium Trail facing back to the broad track you joined a short distance back.

4. Walk a short stretch down Highlands Road. Pass a parking area on your left (trail access to Prior Lake). Immediately past a section with guardrails you will see a blue sign high on a tree for the next segment, McKenzie Creek Trail. Pass barriers and a newer sign. Turn onto this trail, spot a yellow marker on a maple, and two minutes later a blue marker on a large fir. Begin contouring uphill through

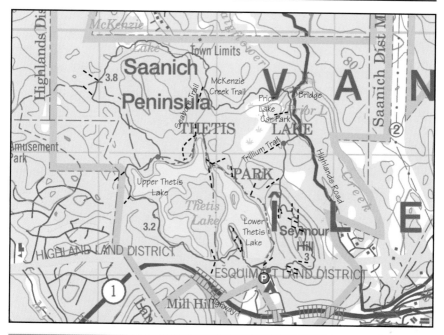

The only high point view on this route is from Seymour Hill and the ridge slightly north (1)

McKenzie Creek (5)

a salal-covered slope with some large firs. You will pass a little side trail on your left down to Prior Lake.

5. After descending, the trail comes to some muddy sections by McKenzie Creek and turns to follow the creek upstream a short distance before crossing a bridge by some lovely little cascades. When you come to a sign for Seaborn Trail, turn right to stay on McKenzie Creek Trail.

6. The trail crosses the creek again and dips away from it before crossing to the left (west) side and passing the south shore of McKenzie Lake (the southwest side of the lake is reedy). Though beautiful, this section can be muddy well into spring. Leaving McKenzie Lake, cross a small stream twice in close succession. The track stays low, with a crest on either side. Ignore two trails heading back on your right until you come to a fork. Head left, still in a slight gully between slopes of rather spindly firs and one sometimes muddy section, until you reach Upper Thetis Lake Trail on the lakeshore.

7. After having wandered the back trails you will find this trail a little like a super-highway full of casual strollers and determined runners. Turn right and follow the shoreline. When you cross a bridge, take the shoreline trail and continue along it over several crests and past a side route with wooden stairs to Phelps Avenue. Carry on until you reach the junction with Trillium Trail.

8. When you reach the signposted junction with Trillium Trail, turn right and go a short distance, and at the next T-junction turn left to rejoin the lakeshore and pass a small swimming beach. As the trail rises toward a high, narrow promontory jutting north into Lower Thetis Lake, you can choose to cut across its base or take the slight detour around its picturesque perimeter.

9. Rejoining the main trail, you will pass a major access to the right leading to the parking lot. Ignore this. Finish off with passing by the main swimming beach before turning back to the parking lot.

Options:

There are too many options to list here. The maze of trails, mapped and unmapped, is huge. If you want to follow the crowds and do a short walk, simply follow the perimeter of the lakes.

On the other hand, if you want to do something epic, you can connect through to two adjoining systems of trails. Francis King Park in the northeast is a well-established area of knolls and a network of short trails. A new area in the northwest leading to Scafe Hill (231 m) appears on maps and looks tempting. Be aware, though, that many of the "trails" are actually old roadbeds, some of which pass through unremarkable scenery. In addition, to reach Scafe Hill it is currently necessary to pass through private land. According to at least one park official, the trails are not yet properly signposted and ready for use.

5. Mount Finlayson

7.4 km loop
High point: 419 m
Height gain: 485 m
Moderate
All year (except if snowy or icy)

Start: Driving west on Highway 1 from Victoria you will pass under the overpass and exits for Sooke and Metchosin. Just over 5 km from there, now heading north, you will come to the well-signposted Goldstream Provincial Park. Don't head for the campground (on the left), but for the Visitor Centre parking area farther up the road on the right.

Difficulty: You will see signs warning of steep cliffs and the inadvisability of bringing children. Much of the trail is in fact rough. It passes sections of heavily eroded, broken rock and then a long section of light scrambling with occasional use of hands. Most of the difficulty comes from the facts that many side tracks criss-cross the main signposted route and that the rock has been worn smooth. Dozens of bright-orange tags have been put on the rock to keep you on track, but it is still surprisingly easy to take a wrong turn unless you make a point of looking out for the next orange marker. Except for a few slightly exposed steps along a ledge, there is no serious exposure anywhere on the main route (though there are dangerous cliffs to the left). Rare icy or snowy conditions can make the trail treacherous.

Although badly infringed on by profit-driven developers, this is still by far the most popular day hike ascent on Vancouver Island. From old-growth forests the broad trail leads to treeless scrambles and, from the summit, views over Victoria and surrounding hills.

1. Walk across the road bridge over the Goldstream River, in October and November pausing to watch the spectacle of the chum salmon spawn. The first section of road and trail has probably the most impressive stands of easily accessible old-growth cedar and Douglas fir outside of Cathedral Grove. A short distance along the road you will see the trailhead and large signs warning of the dangers of the trail up Mt. Finlayson.

2. As soon as you start, the trail splits. Neither route is signposted, but the two rejoin after a short distance. In wet weather, choose to go to the right up the long flight of concrete stairs rather than along the gully-bottom dirt track to the left. If you do turn right, you will be faced with another fork after a short distance along the top of a ridge. A tiny, faded sign on a tree points left toward Mt. Finlayson and, within a few steps, the junction with the alternative route to this point.

3. The broad trail rises over a crest and drops down an amazing network of exposed roots before beginning to climb again, this time over a lot of loose, broken rock. Ignore the track on the right leading past large boulders with faint orange markings (for Bear Mountain subdivision). Very quickly you will reach the beginning of the long section of steep rock climbing, requiring occasional light scrambling. You will quickly pass from virgin forest to scattered Garry oak and arbutus, with increasingly impressive views. Try not to look back at the gigantic housing development and golf course crowding up against the base of the mountain.

4. As the trail approaches the broad, gently rounded top of the mountain, side tracks lead in several directions to viewpoints. Explore these as much as you like, since they all lead back more or less to the summit. Stay well back from the cliffs, though.

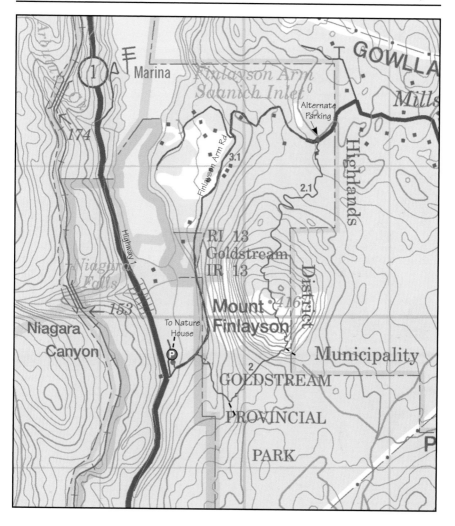

Two old-growth cedars near the trailhead (1)

The San Juan Islands in the U.S., east over the Saanich Peninsula (4)

5. Most visitors return the same way. For a proper little day hike, however, and to enjoy variety and a beautiful wooded trail, carry on right over the summit as the track drops into light forest. At two points the route runs along old road, but otherwise it winds gradually downward on well maintained and easy trails. Earth-and-timber stairs help at a few steeper sections. Toward the end of the route, ignore smaller trails leading off to the right. The trail rises slightly before levelling off and emerging at the road.

6. The final stage of the walk is along asphalt pavement, but don't despair. Finlayson Arm Road is an isolated, twisting, single-lane route that could hardly be quieter or more beautifully forested. The lower it gets, the larger the trees, until, near the end, it passes some truly impressive old-growth giants.

Adjacent trails:

There are many other trails in the park, most of them on the opposite (west) side of the highway. Of these, the trail to Niagara Falls, a small but high cascade, is probably the prettiest. Unfortunately, these don't connect with each other to allow a comfortable loop walk, and they are difficult to approach because of the safety barricades along the busy highway.

The beginning of the steepest section of the trail, near the tree line (3)

6. Gowlland Tod Park
Jocelyn Peak Loop

9.3 km return (partial loop)
High point: 434 m
Height gain: 591 m (cumulative)
Easy / moderate
All season

Almost continuous open ridgewalking amongst arbutus and Garry oak groves. Excellent, airy views of Saanich Inlet.

Start: From Highway 1 some 10 km west from the centre of Victoria, take exit 14 onto Millstream Road. Drive 7 km to Caleb Pike Road. Turn left to the end of the road and the trailhead (600 m).

Difficulty: The trail is somewhat rough underfoot in many places and could be slippery when wet, but otherwise it poses no difficulties.

1. Walk past the sign and slightly downhill to a junction. Turn right in the direction of three signposted destinations: Holmes Peak; McKenzie Bight; and the destination for this day hike, Jocelyn Hill (Jocelyn Peak on some maps). Turning around at Jocelyn Hill or a spot shortly thereafter, rather than carrying on toward McKenzie Bight, gives you the maximum amount of scenic walking with the least change in elevation.

2. After you have gone mostly downhill a little over 500 m you will come to side trails clearly signposted as "closed." Don't be thrown off by the fact that after the second of these a sign now identifies your through route with a new name: "Ridge Top Trail."

When you get to a cleared swath under power lines, you will see a large sign with distances on it and, amongst other things, pointing out that you have come only 800 m to this point (though you will probably feel you've gone much farther). Use this as a chance to gauge your timing. A trail leading straight downhill to your right, under the power lines, is "Holmes Peak Bypass," a shorter option for your return route.

3. The main trail to Holmes Peak takes you past a sequence of excellent viewpoints, the first about 100 m along, and the highest, Holmes Peak, an additional 200 m beyond that. Don't be misled by the term "peak," since this is only a treeless bluff, 329 m high, along a ridge with other similar bluffs.

4. A short distance beyond the viewpoint you will come to a signposted junction. Note the signposted "Holmes Peak Bypass" pointing sharply back to your right, for your return journey, and carry on directly ahead on "Ridge Trail to Jocelyn." When you come to another signposted junction, take the left option toward Jocelyn Hill. Explore the bluffs around Jocelyn Hill a little (434 m).

5. For the loop route, counterintuitively follow the sign for "McKenzie Bight." The trail curves over a crest and heads to the southeast. After winding downhill over mossy crests with glimpses over the forested hills of the "Highlands," the trail enters denser forest. When you come to a signposted junction, turn sharply to the right back toward Ridge Trail via "Timberman Trail." Surprisingly, the route heads roughly back toward Jocelyn Peak but much lower down. Another signposted junction a little later allows you to turn right to rejoin Ridge Trail, or take the left fork to follow a bypass trail roughly parallel to Ridge Trail. Take the right fork to rejoin Ridge Trail.

6. When you reach Ridge Trail, ignore a track to the left that gives an additional loop option. This trail is unattractive, rough and partly overgrown. Instead rejoin Ridge Trail. As you approach Holmes Peak you will have another option: to turn left onto the signposted "Holmes Peak Bypass" for a few hundred metres. This rejoins the ridge trail under the power lines for the last 800 m back to the starting point. The route stays lower and is overall much faster than Ridge Trail, though not quite as attractive, particularly under the power lines.

7. Rejoin the main Ridge Trail all the way back to your starting point.

Options

1. As you will see from the map posted at the trailhead, you can begin your trip with the short trail looping off to the left. Neither the trail nor the viewpoint is nearly as interesting as the main Ridge Trail, to the right. Note, however, that this trail to the left does allow you to make an additional trip to Mt. Finlayson, farther south along the inlet and considerably higher (see the description in Hike 5).

2. While of course it is possible to make McKenzie Bight your destination, at 8.3 km along, be aware that the distances on this particular route seem much greater than the signs indicate. If you decide to do this one-way hike to McKenzie Bight with a two-car shuttle, keep in mind that the only direct vehicle route, via Millstream Lake Road, is along a very narrow, winding road intended for local traffic only. The trail is generally farther away from viewpoints.

3. The loop route to McKenzie Bight itself is described in the companion volume, *Seaside Walks on Vancouver Island*.

A typical section of trail along the higher parts of the ridge (4)

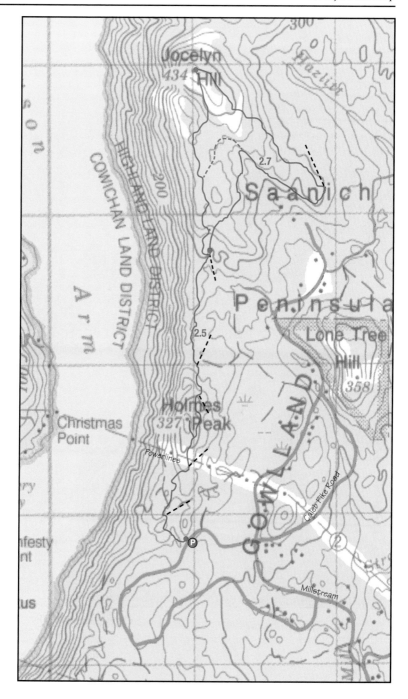

The best views up Saanich Inlet often require leaving the trail a short distance (4)

7. Mount Tzouhalem

Called Cowichan Ridge Trail by locals

5.5 km return
High point: 536 m
Height gain: 510 m
Moderately strenuous
All season

Traversing up the west side of the long Tzouhalem ridge, the clear trail swings back past mossy bluffs and oak meadows to gain the ridgeline of the mountain. The route ascends along this ridge to a sequence of cliffs with magnificent views over the Cowichan Valley and far beyond.

Start: Although it is possible to start at the north end of the trail by St. Ann's Church on Tzouhalem Road, the trail is most attractive and views are best if you start from and return to the south trailhead, at the end of Khenipsen Road. From Highway 1 at 3 km south of Duncan, turn onto Cowichan Bay Road. After 1.6 km, turn left onto Tzouhalem Road for 2.4 km, then right onto Khenipsen Road. At the end of the road, make a U-turn at the paved circle and park in the small gravel lot 50 m back.

Difficulty: A narrow but well-beaten trail with some short sections over bare rock that are slippery in wet weather. There are some unsignposted side tracks to be avoided, but the main through route is more or less obvious.

1. Finding the start of this trail is a little daunting because it is not signposted, and you will get the impression you'll have to ignore a whole battery of signs warning you about entering private property. To find the trailhead, go to the very end of the turnaround area and walk a few metres down the road to the right. Next, fork left onto a gravel drive, currently posted with a handmade sign saying "The Bumpy Road."

2. A few metres along, this gravel road heads downhill. Fork left onto a broad track more or less traversing the slope. About 30 m along, again fork left onto a wide trail. This track follows an old roadbed for about 500 m. It ends with an interesting structure of precariously balanced rocks indicating the beginning of the narrow trail.

3. The narrow path traverses a fairly steep bank through forest, gradually becoming a little rougher underfoot. When you come to the first of two open areas of mossy rock, you will have attractive views across Cowichan Bay, framed by weathered fir and arbutus. Just beyond the bluffs the trail forks. The branch to the right, heading downhill, is a beautiful walk, with some "rock garden" configurations of arbutus, mossy rocks and wildflowers, but it leads only to some houses in the village of Genoa Bay about 1 km away. For the route up the mountain, take the left fork. In essence this is the spot where the trail begins to swing back along the ridge, first by heading more steeply uphill through some areas of oak and meadows.

4. After a few minutes you will pass a small path leading to the left off the main trail. This is the first of several such side tracks, all comparatively small. The main route, tending uphill, is clear. Beside one of these trails, branching right, you will see a small piece of plywood nailed to a tree. This is the path going to Genoa Bay and the houses there.

After climbing over a section of bare rock, the trail enters the forest again to bring you, for the first time, to the centre of the ridge. Look for a striking old Douglas fir with a huge bent limb. Immediately to its left is a small trail taking you to a magnificent

The view over Quamichan Lake towards the snow-clad peaks of the Island Range. (6)

viewpoint, this time facing east instead of west. You will be looking beyond Stony Hill and across Sansum Narrows to the two high points of Salt Spring Island, Mt. Maxwell and to its right, Mt. Bruce.

5. From this point the trail climbs along the top of the ascending ridge, through meadows and old firs. After climbing over an open area of bluffs, scarred with invasive and largely dead broom plants, you will have a 180 degree view to the south, extending from Salt Spring Island on the left, south to Saanich Inlet and west to the Island Range. Entering the forest again, the trail passes below a cliffy area and a frog pond. It switchbacks fairly steeply upward to gain the top of the ridge again. Before long you will see a wide dirt track coming in from the right. From this point

on, the ridge trail intersects at several points with similar tracks, all part of an elaborate mountain-biking system that covers the north end of the peak.

6. By keeping left you will come to a series of impressive cliff viewpoints, all looking over the Cowichan Valley and the Island Range beyond. Where the cliff edge trail begins a descent into a gully you will probably want to turn back and make your way to your starting point.

Option:

If you've brought two vehicles and have arranged a shuttle, you can carry on to the northwest end of the trail by St. Ann church on Tzouhalem Road. Be aware, though, that you will get the best range of views and most isolated part of the trail by turning back.

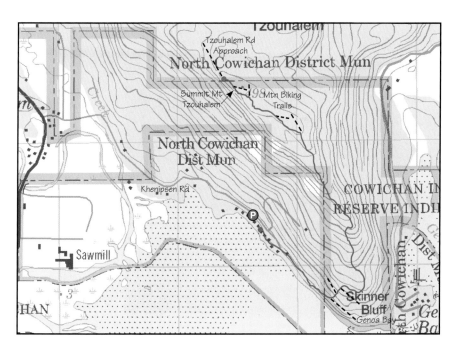

View south from the first section of open bluffs before the trail swings north onto the ridge (3)

The trail along the ridge runs through some lovely areas of moss, fir and Garry oak (5)

8. Maple Mountain

11.4 km partial loop
High point: 505 m
Height gain: 306 m (plus many
   small ups and downs)
Moderate
All season (though there may be
   snow at the top in winter)

From ravines of large cedars and swordferns to high, mossy bluffs with great views of Sansum Narrows and Salt Spring Island and, from the top, Maple Bay and Mt. Tzouhalem.

Start: From Highway 1 almost 4 km north of downtown Duncan, turn right onto Herd Road. After 5.8 km, when you see the sign for the Crofton ferry, turn left onto Osborne Bay Road for 3.5 km. Turn right onto Chilco Road and follow it to the turnaround at its end. (Don't be put off by the "No Exit" sign.) Park so as not to block the yellow gate, which is usually locked.

Difficulty: This is a safe but generally narrow path with no exposure. It can require careful footing on some sections of irregular rock outcroppings and along stretches that are slippery with mud and moss during the winter or after heavy rains.

1. Walk past the yellow gate barring the gravel road until you see a blue "Trail" sign on the right pointing to the left along an old roadbed. On your left you will see another blue trail sign and several splashes of blue paint on tree trunks. You will be following this "blue trail" for a few kilometres as it roughly parallels the shoreline and gradually approaches it.

2. Very quickly you will come to a dirt road. Turn right and, a few steps along, take a right fork, following a blue sign and a rough placard saying "To Cross." In two minutes you will come to the beginning of the trail proper and a sign warning that you are entering a Municipal Forest Reserve and should watch for unmarked hazards. The next section of the trail dips and rises through some stands of large cedars and swordferns across some small ravines and streambeds.

3. You will come to a photogenic log bridge and small cascading falls just before a junction with the "yellow" trail leading off to your left. Go straight ahead on the "blue" trail. Along this section you will ascend to about 230 m, then begin descending, partly by way of some switchbacking trails with some viewpoints from a mossy bluff. One of these has a rough religious cross.

4. When, much later, you come to a four-way intersection, turn right to join a path marked with pink ribbon. The trail angles fairly steeply uphill along an old track. Ignore a tempting-looking trail marked with pink ribbon and branching off to the right. Carry on straight ahead up the old track, where you will soon pick up more pink ribbon. You will also soon see that that right-hand fork you didn't take now rejoins your route, but over a largely collapsed log bridge.

5. After a considerable uphill section, you will come to a broad service road (370 m). After a few steps along this road you will see the clearly marked "pink" trail entering the forest. Ascending another 100 m over the next section will bring you again to the service road. Note where the pink-ribboned trail swings back into the trees; but to reach the summit viewpoint, leave the trail and head along the service road for about 100 m.

6. After enjoying the view from this end of your walk, return to the point where the pink-ribboned trail enters the trees, and descend fairly steeply to a junction with the "blue" trail. The junction is a

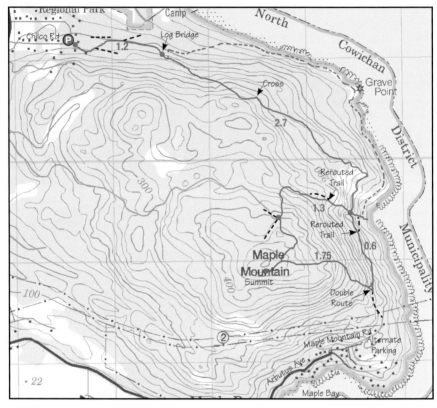

The "yellow" trail runs along rocky bluffs mostly near the shore (O)

little confusing because there are two spots where you can turn left to begin contouring back northward. In fact, however, these two options are only a few metres apart (though not visible simultaneously) and both converge.

7. The "blue" route – back to the point where you left it to climb to the summit via the "pink" trail – is mostly clear and straightforward, though it does require a little care at a couple of narrow rocky spots. In addition you will encounter one place just before the intersection with the "pink" trail where an older, clearly disused version of the "blue" trail drops away to the right. It is actually usable, but not as good as the newer version. Both converge after a short distance.

8. Having reached the intersection with the "pink" route, carry on straight ahead to return the way you came.

Option:

If you want variety on your return and are happy to add about a kilometre to the overall distance, you can turn right at this last intersection to carry on downhill a short way and pick up the "yellow" trail (actually yellow-green at some points) on your left. The "yellow" trail is fairly rough in places and can be indistinct when it crosses open bluffs, but it does give some beautiful, open views. At three points you can descend fairly easily to little stony pocket beaches. As the path swings away from the water it crosses a broad track that might be mistaken for the through route. Cross this wide track and pick up the yellow flagging to keep on the route until you rejoin the "blue" trail just before the log bridge. Most of this hike is described in more detail in the companion volume, *Seaside Walks on Vancouver Island.*

From the summit, the view extends all the way to the Saanich Peninsula (5)

This little cascade near the beginning of the trail dries to a trickle during a hot summer (3)

9. *Skutz Falls Loop*

6.4 km loop
High point: 123 m
Height gain: 23 m
Easy
All season

A loop trail over a dizzyingly high historic trestle. Canyon-top views of deep, green river pools, rapids and some magnificent old firs.

Start: From Highway 1 at 4 km north of Duncan, turn west onto Highway 18, signposted for Cowichan Lake. After 19 km, turn left onto Skutz Falls Road for just 50 m, then left again onto Cowichan Lake Road for 700 m and right onto Mayo Road for 2.7 km. Turn left onto Riverbottom Road and go a little over 1.5 km to "Mile 66 Trestle Day Use Area." (Don't be confused by any directions to "Stoltz Pool," a similar name but a different part of the park.)

Difficulty: The trail is generally well defined and has only a few sections of fairly steep but still quite easy ascents and descents. Although some drops near the track are precipitous and potentially dangerous, the trail itself is safe. The south shore of the route is thick with protruding roots but otherwise fairly easy. Blue and white markers on trees, the occasional sign, a few small boardwalks and some guardrails increase the safety.

1. From the parking lot the broad gravel trail curves down to a developed park area with an outhouse and, after a few metres, comes to the former Mile 66 Trestle, now a wide boardwalk with high railings. Parents of small children will be reassured by the wire netting, since the trestle, about 90 m long, is a dizzying 35 m above the canyon bottom.

2. Turn right and follow the clear trail more or less along the rim of the canyon, some of it along an almost ridge-like formation. The route then dips a little inland, crossing a bridge and a boardwalk. After traversing an open grassy area with the only Garry oaks on this side of the river, the trail descends fairly steeply. Almost immediately you will come to a side track that allows the only easy access to the shore on this side of the river. An interestingly stratified outcropping juts into the fast-rushing water. This is a good place for a picnic or a pause. Thereafter the trail runs along the top of a bank back from the river's edge, through relatively small firs.

3. After switchbacking up a moderately steep grade and traversing a section of heavily eroded gravel canyonside, the trail reaches viewpoints with a guardrail, then drops, again quite steeply, to a bank only a few metres above the river. The forest along this section is mostly small firs.

4. This segment ends when you come to a gravelled forest service road, signposts and a newly upgraded bridge over the river. Cross the bridge, noting the fine views up and down the stream. Skutz Falls itself is really just rapids. After crossing the bridge, go a few metres along the gravel road to find a path turning down toward the river. This trail runs close to and slightly above the riverbank, occasionally close to the edge of quite a steep drop. Look for patches of camas lilies and larkspur in late spring and early summer. This section ends in an open area with easy access to the river and a bare, rocky promontory into fast-rushing water. In summer expect to see inner-tubers!

5. Here the trail turns away from the river through a plain of big, mossy maples and emerges at a large open area, the Horseshoe Bend campground. You will see several tent pads and other camping facilities here (including a pump), but this area is intended for overnight campers rather than day visitors.

Maple trees in autumn near the west end of Marie Canyon's north shore. Autumn can be an excellent time to visit the river because of the many big leaf maples (6)

6. The last part of the trail is the highlight of the whole route. Climbing to the edge of Marie Canyon, the path winds amongst many large old firs and has several magnificent viewpoints over deep, green pools of amazingly clear water and short sections of rapids. Striking cliffs and stratified, rocky shore edge the canyon. Be careful not to venture too far out onto some of the user-made viewpoints jutting over the canyon's edge.

Option:

After crossing the road bridge by Skutz Falls, if you have an appetite for a longer walk, turn upstream before turning downstream. A comparatively rough, user-made fishing trail carries on for several kilometres along the north bank of the river, first past interesting fish ladders (where there is an additional road access).

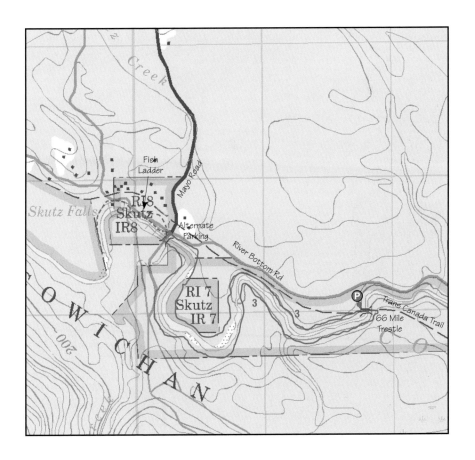

Interestingly stratified rock at the most convenient shore access side trail on the south bank (2)

Looking north from the high viewpoint nearing the west end of the south bank (3)

10. Cowichan River Footpath

Length: 32 km return (feels much shorter and there are shorter options)
High point: 120 m
Height gain: 200 m (cumulative over many small ups and downs)
Easy / moderate (long)
All season

Start: From Highway 1 just south of Duncan, turn west onto Allenby Road for 350 m. Turn left onto Koksilah Road for another 700 m, then take the second right onto Miller Road for 500 m. Next, make a right onto Glenora Road for 4 km. Take a slight right onto Vaux Road for 2.2 km, then a right onto Robertson Road. Continue until you see signposts for the Holt Creek trailhead of the Cowichan River Trail.

Difficulty: Most of the path is well maintained and easy. Some of the boardwalks are slippery when wet. All streams are bridged. The northern section is next to dangerous cliffs but the trail itself is safe.

Huge maples, cottonwoods and cedars along a well-developed trail near or beside a broad, fast-rushing river.

Note that the distances on the map are stated in terms of the signs posted along the trail.

1. Follow the broad, level track (300 m) to a point where other paths branch off. The trail to the right goes to Glenora Riverside Park, the one to the left to a picnic shelter and other day park facilities (in sight) and beyond that the rails-to-trails Trans Canada Trail.

2. Keep straight ahead till you see a sign saying you have come 650 m from the Holt Creek trailhead. Keep straight ahead on the kind of rooty path you will be following the rest of the way. When you come to a prominent 1 km marker, you will see another sign, this one pointing down a side track to the Glenora trailhead. Ignore this, and keep straight ahead in the direction of Holt Creek and the Skutz Falls trailhead, marked as 20 km distant.

3. Descend the high bank via a series of stairs and a reinforced pathway and follow along the short distance to the Holt Creek bridge, a good spot to watch spawning salmon in October and November. Once you have crossed the bridge you will come almost immediately to a split in the trail, accompanied by a map and a sign indicating that both branches join after about 1.5 km. In order to follow the river, take the right fork.

4. The trail runs fairly close to the riverbank, over roots of large trees, then heads away from the main stream to a kind of backwater. After climbing a little, you arrive at a signpost indicating the 3 km mark and the convergence with the trail you left 1.5 km back. Puzzlingly, the sign says the Skutz Falls trailhead is still 20 km distant, though you have walked almost 2 km from the previous such sign!

5. After running along the top of a bank for about 150 m, the trail descends to near the main river until it comes upon another tributary. You will pass a historic "stump bridge" and a signposted riverside picnic area just before coming to the 4 km marker.

6. Crossing "Rickie Dickie" bridge and traversing up and away from the river, you will come to a 5 km sign and a short path leading up to the Trans Canada Trail. The next section, through private property until the 6 km marker, keeps largely to the slope immediately below the Trans Canada Trail. The trail crosses an open swath of land under power lines just before you reach the 7 km mark.

45

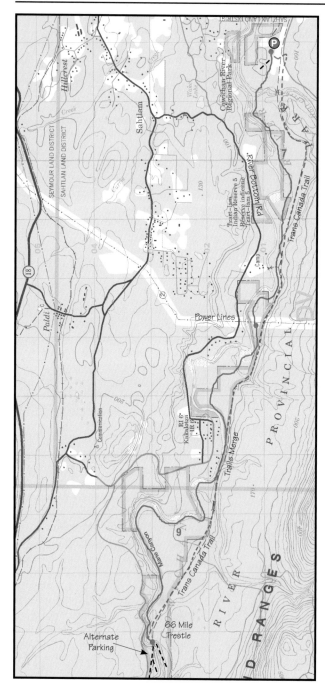

Rich displays of moss cover the maples in the shadier parts of the trail's east end (4)

Mile 66 Trestle, the turn around spot for this route, is a remarkable piece of engineering (9)

7. Expect several boardwalks and an intriguing sign for "Bear Hollow" just before reaching an attractive riverbank section. As the route turns inland and climbs a hill you will find a sign saying you have come 8.6 km from the trailhead. Somewhat later the path merges with the Trans Canada Trail for the next kilometre. When you get to the separation of the two trails, you will notice that the signed distances for Mile 66 Trestle via the Trans Canada Trail is only 2.8 km, while it is 5 km via the river trail. Turn toward the river trail.

8. After passing a lagoon-like backwater off the main river and after the 12 km sign, the trail comes to the river's edge and later to a wide meadow (also accessible from the Trans Canada Trail). Be careful if you are tempted to linger and picnic here: the bank drops precipitously to the river.

9. The trail is mostly close to the riverbank, next to overhanging cedars, until midway between the 14 and 15 km signs, where it rises significantly. The last, particularly scenic section is along the edge of Marie Canyon. The trail here has spectacular views into the deep gorge, where the river is forced into chutes and rapids between its narrow banks. When you get to Mile 66 Trestle, where the Trans Canada Trail crosses the canyon, walk to the centre of the trestle for great views up and down the canyon.

10. Return the way you came if you are up for the full 32 km hike.

Options:

1. If you are getting short of time or energy you can return to your starting point via the Trans Canada Trail. This will save you several kilometres, and of course the walking is easier, though less interesting. After crossing the Holt Creek trestle, you know you are nearing the turnoff to reach the Holt Creek trailhead (and nearby Glenora Riverside Park).

2. You can arrange a pickup at the parking area for Mile 66 Trestle (signposted from Riverbottom Road).

Opposite: A particularly beautiful viewpoint in Marie Canyon, near the west end of the trail (9)

11. Stocking Lake and Heart Lake

9.5 km loop (plus 500 m side trail
  to viewpoint)
High point: 390 m
Height gain: 285 m (plus many
  short ascents and descents)
Moderate
All season

A loop route, partly on abandoned roads, past two pristine wilderness lakes, one with great swimming. Two good viewpoints, one of them from the top of a ridge over Ladysmith Harbour and nearby Gulf Islands.

Start: On the southern outskirts of Ladysmith, turn off Highway 1 at the traffic lights onto Davis Road (by the Dairy Queen). Following Davis Road steadily uphill, turn right onto Battie Drive and park in a gravel lot a few metres along on the right. Walk less than a block up Battie Drive to a Y-junction with Ryan Place, where you will see a "Trail" post and a yellow gate at the beginning of a trail leading uphill into forest.

Difficulty: Much of this route is along old roadbeds which are severely eroded at steep sections. Loose, jagged boulders can be hard on ankles. Sections close to Heart Lake can have muddy potholes well into summer. The trail along the south shore of Stocking Lake likewise has several rough sections. Split-log bridges help with some small streams. The complicated route is well supplied with signposts and a few maps, but there are a few confusing junctions.

This loop trail is best walked clockwise because the more attractive of the two lakes then comes second. In addition, once you have gone more than halfway you are in a better position to judge whether you want to make the extra effort to climb to the viewpoint not directly on the trail. You can then choose to shorten your return by following the option described below.

1. Walk past the "Trail" post and the yellow gate and up the gravel road a short distance to another T-junction. Turn left to follow the "purple" Stocking Lake route. Carry along this gravel track under power lines to reach a new subdivision road. Turn right and go 75 m, then left at the signposted entrance to a broad gravel track entering the forest, past a yellow gate.

2. After curves and gradual ascent, this broad part of the road comes to an end by a reservoir and another gate. Here the road narrows and becomes more attractively like a broad trail rising through second growth. After a short distance, when you come to an unsignposted fork, you can go either way, since the two tracks later converge.

3. The trail contours around a high crest on your right. After significant curves, it opens out somewhat over a clear-cut area with good views to the east and southeast over rolling tracts of forest and across the water to Salt Spring Island. Re-entering the forest, the road drops, crosses a little stream and then begins rising steadily again until you are close to Stocking Lake. When you come to a T-junction, turn right, pass a yellow gate and go a few minutes along a potholed track until you come to an unsignposted split. The two routes connect within a few metres. If you turn right you come to the significant, signposted junction that will bring you back to this point after your circuit.

4. Turn left and drop back down the slope to enjoy the views of Stocking Lake. Head straight ahead along the dirt trail. This beautiful section dips and rises behind a lattice of trees along the shady south shore of the lake.

5. Crossing a small log bridge at the end

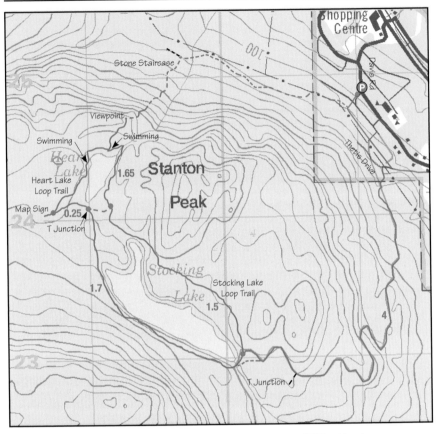

The view over Ladysmith Harbour, Yellow Point, to Thetis and Valdes islands (7)

of the lake, carry on straight ahead along a pleasant, smooth track, passing a 6 km sign, until you get to a T-junction. Turn left and in a short time you will come to an open, gravel area with a map posted. Barely visible up the track to the right is the Heart Lake signpost you want.

6. This heavily rutted and often muddy track will bring you close to and then along the shore of perfect little Heart Lake. Various small trails interlace toward the north end of the lake, all of which keep you en route as long as you stay close to the lake. The best swimming spots are by a campsite along the west shore and off the rocky bluff at the north end.

7. After your dip, take a brief detour directly away from the water along the trail leading uphill from the rocky bluff at the north end of the lake to the viewpoint. It is a short distance to the highpoint, but you will have to go a few minutes beyond this to drop down to the bluff with its magnificent views over Ladysmith harbour and Thetis and Valdes islands.

8. Returning to the lake, turn left to follow the beautiful little trail running roughly parallel to the east shore and coming to a T-junction with a broad dirt track. Turn left and you are on the return leg of the Stocking Lake loop trail. You will catch only glimpses of the lake from the irregular and potholed track.

9. At the head of Stocking Lake you will rejoin your initial route. Return the way you came.

Option:

If you wish to avoid retracing any of your outward route and cut off considerable distance, keep on past the viewpoint above Heart Lake. The steeply descending trail switchbacks over rock steps and roots. At several points a steeper trail cuts off and re-joins the less steep route. This steep section ends with a set of concrete and stone steps. Once you join a broad track, turn right and follow the comparatively featureless, easy track as it contours the ridge and gradually descends to the original T-junction where you began your loop by turning left.

A typical section of trail on the south shore trail of Stocking Lake

The first viewpoint on the west shore of Heart Lake, looking toward the swimming bluff on the north shore, and behind it the rise to the viewpoint (6)

12. Holland Creek

6.4 km loop
High point: 150 m
Height gain: 125 m
Easy
All season

Broad, well-maintained loop trail through a beautifully forested ravine and past a pretty waterfall. Side trail to hillside viewpoint over Ladysmith Harbour.

Start: From Highway 1 southbound from Ladysmith, turn right onto Davis Road and immediately right again into Coronation Mall. The trail leaves from the highway side of the Safeway supermarket. Respect the mall businesses by buying a few snacks or drinks to take with you on your walk.

Difficulty: The trail on the south bank of Holland Creek is more strenuous than its north bank counterpart. Boardwalks, bridges and handrails make the going easy, however. The side route to the Rotary Viewpoint is a little rougher with some loose gravel, but still easy. The loop is a favourite jogging trail for locals.

1. Walk along the highway side of the Safeway store and descend a broad gravel path toward Holland Creek. Ignore a track leading to the left, signposted to a ballpark, and instead cross a small bridge and turn left to follow the south bank of the creek. The first part of the trail rises well above the streambed and crosses Dogwood Drive (another possible starting point).

2. Cross the parking lot and descend toward the stream, crossing another bridge. Between here and the power lines the trail crosses a sturdy boardwalk and a bridge, while rising and falling a little, then climbs a wooden staircase and passes the 1 km post.

3. For the most part the trail stays amongst tall trees well above the creek until you come to a striking viewpoint of Crystal Falls. The last section, after the falls and to the bridge, becomes a broad, road-width track and the high point of the first leg of the trip. You will come to a utility building and a signpost pointing the way to Heart Lake (see Hike 11).

4. Cross the bridge, and to take the detour to Rotary Viewpoint, climb the stone steps and turn right along the clear dirt path. Ignore the several side trails, though most of them rejoin the main trail. At the high point you will find a picnic table and a good view over Ladysmith, the harbour and Thetis Island.

5. Back at the bridge junction, you may choose to return the way you came if you want the most natural scenery. To make a loop, turn left down the stream. On this side the trail is generally higher above the creek and both smoother and broader. You will pass one of two old dams dating from the days of coal industry activity here and shortly thereafter a fork in the trail up to the Mackie Road parking lot. Some of the prettiest views of the creek (as well as of the second historical dam) come during the next short section before a second exit trail, this one to the Sixth Avenue parking area (and washrooms).

6. After a sterile section of trail near some houses, you will come to the 5 km signpost and the beginning of perhaps the most attractive section of the whole hike. The trail descends some dramatic stairs and arrives at the creekside. Here you will find pleasant pools and good picnic/resting spots.

7. Near the end of the trail you will see one fork to the left leading up to Dogwood Drive on the north side of the creek. To return to the trailhead, take the right fork

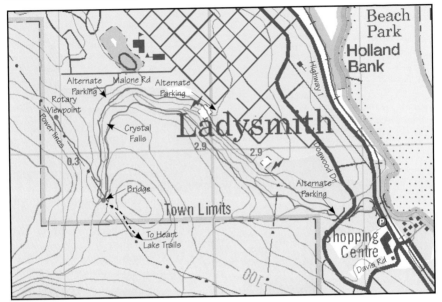

The easiest and prettiest approaches to the creek are near the end of the loop route (5)

and, once across Dogwood Drive, rejoin the trail you followed up to Dogwood Drive in the first place.

Option:

The fairly steep trail to Heart Lake begins near the bridge at the top end of the loop.

The trail is 3 km each way and is well signposted except at its beginning along a branching gravel road. Heart Lake is pretty and surprisingly isolated for being close to town. Hike 11 describes a longer loop to the lake starting south of Ladysmith.

The trail along the north shore has several impressive staircases from the top of the high bank (5)

The footbridge over Holland Creek for the loop route (4)

Crystal Falls and a beautiful display of maidenhair ferns on the mossy cliff (3)

From the Rotary viewpoint, the view over Ladysmith harbour to Thetis and Galiano islands (4)

13. *Haslam Trail to Timberland Lake*

7 km return (with longer options)
High point: 235 m
Height gain: 150 m
Easy
All season

The chief attractions of this trail are the dramatic creek gorge with its suspension bridge near one end of the trail and the attractive, warm lake at the other. The walk between, on the Trans Canada Trail, is mostly on abandoned logging roads.

Start: From Highway 1 about 15 km south of downtown Nanaimo, near the south end of Cassidy Airport, turn onto Timberlands Road and follow it to its end. To reach the actual trailhead, you will have to ignore the "No Entry" signs and follow the small "Trans Canada Trail" signs posted along 1.3 km of gravel road after the pavement ends. The trailhead is marked with a sign but it is not always easy to see. Look for large boulders and a broad trail beside a fence.

Difficulty: The route is well signposted with blue and white "Haslam Trail" signs. Part of the steep track from the creek end of the trail to the higher land can be wet, rutted and made uncomfortable with loose, jagged gravel. Side trails by the gorge can be dangerous when wet. Keep to the main track. Otherwise, the only difficulty will be felt by those with vertigo as they cross the spectacular (and slightly bouncy!) suspension bridge.

1. The trailhead is a gap in the foliage to the left of a fence. The trail itself, a little rough in sections, is nevertheless clear. It follows the fence, first to the edge of the treed creek canyon and then along the edge of the canyon to a small set of wood and dirt steps and the spectacular suspension bridge. The bridge, about 40 m long, is about 15 m above the rapids rushing through the narrow gorge.

2. Once across the bridge you will see small user-made trails dropping down the steep bank toward the creek. These are potentially dangerous, particularly when wet. Carry on along the main trail, past signs, to meet a gravel road. A blue

and white sign with an arrow points you left (though there is an alternative route to the right).

3. This roadbed, the signposted Trans Canada Trail route, runs parallel to the creek below a logged-off slope. The mountain framed by the view is Mt. Benson, Nanaimo's iconic peak. About 1 km along, the road narrows and begins a fairly steep climb. (If you wish, you could make an interesting detour en route to this spot. Instead of following the arrows for this first 1 km, fork left down a narrow roadbed about 500 m from the junction with the suspension bridge trail. A narrow track runs beside the creek until it reaches an attractive creekside spot about 500 m along. You can rejoin the Trans Canada Trail by retracing your steps a little and making your way up another short track the few metres to the main gravel road and the Trans Canada Trail.)

4. The only steep part of the route, a rutted roadbed through some attractive forest, climbs almost 100 m during the next 300 m. After levelling off in a cleared area with some pleasant mountain views, it merges with another track from the right. A blue and white sign points your way.

5. The rest of the way to Timberland Lake is roughly level, through second-growth forest. Follow the signs for "Haslam Trail" past two more merging tracks, the first from the left, the second from the right.

6. When you glimpse Timberland Lake through a few firs, leave the through route

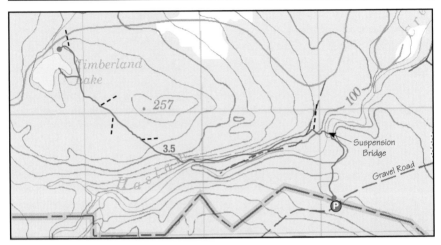

The Trans Canada Trail is intended for cyclists as well as hikers, here on the bluffs on the south shore. This is one of two favourite swimming spots (6)

and take either of two parallel, rough and rutted dirt tracks to the left to arrive at an open area of rounded conglomerate rock, one of the two most popular spots for picnicking and swimming.

7. To reach the other best picnic and swim spot, follow the dirt track back to the main Trans Canada Trail route and follow it along the north side of the lake. Follow the signs to a small clearing where, in midsummer, you can easily get into some of the warmest swimming water you will ever experience.

8. Return by the same route.

Options

If you wish to go farther along the Trans Canada Trail route, follow the signs past this lakeside spot and cross a main gravel road, where you will see a sign labelled "White Pine Trail." From here to the Spruston Road trailhead the route first follows roadbeds and then a forest path with little change of elevation. A shuttle pickup can be arranged for this end, since the roads to the trailhead are good. Because no bridge has yet been built over the Nanaimo River, there is no connection with the Trans Canada Trail on the north side of the river.

The striking footbridge viewed from the west bank (1)

The Haslam Creek canyon narrows downstream, creating a sequence of rapids and deep pools (1)

14. Extension Ridge: "The Abyss"

12 km return
High point: 281 m
Height gain: 208 m
Moderate
All season

A largely forested walk that starts in a suburban park before becoming remote. Ascent to an unusual rift ("abyss") on an exposed meadow of conglomerate rock, followed by a ridgetop trail with views over Nanaimo.

Start: From Highway 19 bypassing Nanaimo, turn east onto Fifth Street for 850 m, then right onto Wakesiah Avenue for 260 m. Take the first right onto Nanaimo Lakes Road for 750 m and enter the signposted parking lot for Colliery Dam Park.

Difficulty: The first part of the trail is extremely easy, on a gradual uphill asphalt track. Thereafter the route is along a forest trail that has protruding roots and a few muddy sections in winter, but with generally good grip over rough areas of conglomerate rock.

1. Walk through the parking lot, past the washrooms and along the top of the historic dam with the small recreational lake behind it. (There are controversial plans, temporarily suspended as at fall 2013, to remove the dam.) Follow the paved trail through the forest, gradually heading uphill until its end on Harewood Mines Road.

2. Walk along Harewood Mines Road under Highway 19 and turn right onto the small dirt path into the forest. Follow this gradual uphill trail, ignoring the occasional small side path. Descend a long flight of sturdy wooden steps. The trail ends under power lines. Turn left and cross the road.

3. The next section is ugly but short. Spot the Trans Canada Trail marker by some concrete barriers and go a short way along a rutted gravel road until you see a blue and white sign pointing to the right, up a set of wood and gravel steps.

Turn right past a rutted roadbed leading left. Within a few metres you will come to another small blue and white sign and, under a pylon, the beginning of the path leading off to the left. A large sign indicates the beginning of the "Extension Ridge" section of the Trans Canada Trail.

4. Climb fairly steeply, crossing some areas of bare conglomerate rock. Although the trail forks, the routes soon rejoin. Near the top of the ridge the trail crosses a nearly circular area of moss and rock. Cutting through this is the "abyss," a deep rift in the otherwise solid dome of sandstone rock. Apparently created by the earthquake of 1946, the "bottomless" abyss, about 40 cm wide, has one edge lower than the other by about 40 cm.

5. From this point the trail leads more or less along the highest part of the ridge, gradually ascending over bumps of conglomerate rock through a light forest of fir and arbutus. You will come to an open area with a power line structure and a great view over the south end of Nanaimo, the harbour, Duke Point and Gabriola Island. Shortly after you enter the trees, ignore a trail to the right marked with a rough sign saying "Poker Run."

6. When you come to an open area with a peculiar rock circle decorated with toys and figurines, ignore an (unsignposted) trail called "The Connector" leading off to the left. A blue and white sign points straight ahead. Ignoring other small side paths, reach the end of the ridge. A set of wood and dirt steps leads to a narrow gravel service road and a large sign indicating this to be the entrance for the

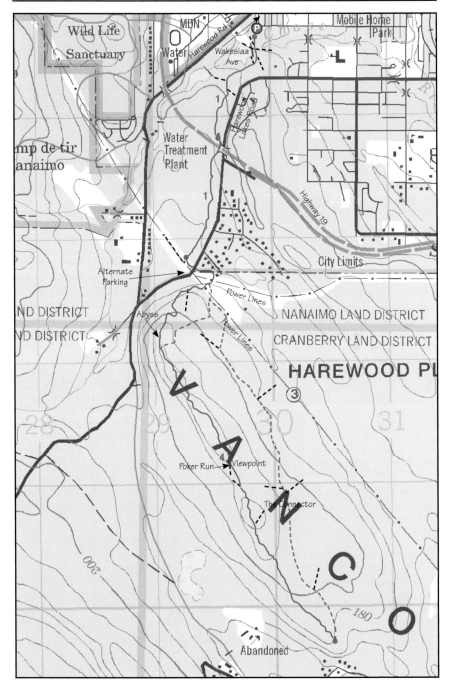

Extension Ridge trail for those approaching via the gravel road.

7. Return the way you came.

Options:

1. If you come during the end of April or in May, consider climbing up to the ridge not by way of the main trail but via an old roadbed to the left of the trail. Although ATVs occasionally chew up the meadows of wildflowers, if they have been restrained in their destruction, you can feast your eyes on colourful displays of sea blush, camas lilies and other wildflowers. When you come to a fork, turn right to walk through patches of meadow and sprinkled trees to join the main trail at the top of the ridge. You will join the ridge trail about 75 m west of the locally famous "abyss," but you can visit this feature on the return leg.

2. At the southeast end of the ridge it is possible to carry on for many more kilometres along the route designated as the "Trans Canada Trail." First, though, you would need to walk about 1.5 km along a sequence of uninspiring residential streets before reaching the trailhead for the "Pipeline" section of the trail.

3. It is possible to make a slightly faster return to your car by turning left onto the gravel road at the end of the trail and following a series of rough roadbeds, first to the power lines and then along them. This route is not as attractive as a return trip along the ridge trail.

4. Shorter versions of the hike can be done by starting immediately after passing under Highway 19 and parking on the (slightly cramped) shoulder of the road or by continuing up Harewood Mines Road to the power lines and the parking area by the Trans Canada Trail head.

The so-called "abyss," an impressive crack in an exposed section of sandstone near the high point of Extension Ridge (4)

One of several rounded bluffs of sandstone that the trail crosses (4)

The sandstone and conglomerate rock make the trail along the ridge excellent for mountain biking. The trail is equally popular with joggers and walkers (6)

The comparatively rare "Lady Slipper" can be found at a few spots along the trail in spring

15. *Mount Benson*

7 km return
High point: 1023 m
Height gain: 726 m
Moderate / strenuous
April to November

Nanaimo's iconic and much-loved local playground with great views over Nanaimo Harbour, Newcastle, Protection and Gabriola islands.

Start: From Nanaimo Parkway (Highway 19), turn onto the northwest end of the Jingle Pot Road loop (near Mostar Road). After 4.7 km turn right onto Kilpatrick Road for 1.7 km. Next, turn onto Benson View Road and carry on until you see a Mt. Benson Regional Park sign on the left with a roadside gravel parking area.

Difficulty: The route here is more or less continuously uphill with "steps" amongst roots and rocks. Because these are user-made tracks rather than official park trails, they are comparatively steep and direct, but also, some would say, more satisfying to walk on than park-style trails. Hands will be useful at a few spots, but even the steepest sections aren't quite "scrambling."

Probably the main difficulty is keeping on track, since there are several interlacing routes, some of them the remnants of extreme mountain-biking trails, mostly fading now. Increasing numbers of markers help keep you on course. Since becoming a regional park, the area has increasing numbers of signs. The trail is used all year, by ski and snowshoe enthusiasts in winter and by hikers and bikers in summer.

1. From the west end of the parking lot, a broad, clear trail leads over a floating bridge across Witchcraft Lake. Turn right along the wide, level path parallel to the lakeshore. You will see a sign for Witchcraft Trail, a route that starts up the mountain a little farther along the horizontal trail. For the route described here, carry on until you see a side trail and an orange blaze on a tree.

2. The trail leads fairly steeply uphill

past some large firs, passing an impressive, fern-covered cliff. Ignore any small side trails feeding in from below. In essence the trail goes up three giant steps before tending to the right. Pause at an attractive, open bluff with good views before carrying on, again tending rightward. Orange markers begin lining the path.

3. You will come to a large junction marked with a handmade sign reading "Way Down" and pointing both along the trail you have just come on and another trail to the left. A few steps on uphill you will see a handmade, mountain-shaped sign. You will soon come to a fork with two more handmade signs, one pointing to a viewpoint on the left, the other straight ahead to the summit of Mt. Benson. Unless you wish to use the viewpoint as a turn-around spot, go straight ahead to the better ones higher up.

4. A few minutes more brings you to another fork in the trail and another sign, this one being the painted image of a mountain pointing to the left. At the next fork follow the orange markers to the right (though the trail to the left soon rejoins the main track). A little later you come to another fork. Both trails have orange markers and rejoin a little farther along, although a sign saying "Mt. Benson" points to the right fork.

5. You will soon emerge on the remnant of an old logging road. A small regional park map is posted here. As you can see from the map, you can elect to turn right onto an old roadbed and take a wide loop, or continue straight ahead. The latter route is more attractive and not especially

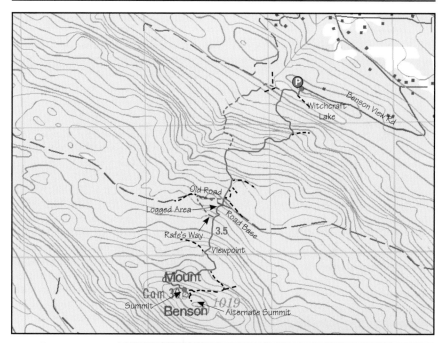

Benson View Rd
Witchcraft Lake
Old Road
Logged Area
Road Base
Rafe's Way
3.5
Viewpoint
Mount
Com 3083
Summit
Benson
1019
Alternate Summit

Stonecrop gives a colourful blaze to the summit ridge throughout the latter part of the summer

steep. You will come to a small logged area with lots of fireweed in the summer and a view of Nanaimo Harbour. Cross this and pick up the forest trail leading up a dirt bank.

6. After a few minutes the trail opens out onto a much broader gravel track. Here you will see a Nanaimo Regional District sign saying "Rafe's Way" and one arrow pointing left, "To Summit," and another to the right, "Way Down." This descent route is the old roadbed circling around to the junction described in paragraph 5 just above. Red plastic patches nailed to trees make your route finding easy from this spot all the way to the summit.

7. Follow the red-marked trail as it becomes increasingly steep and narrow until you climb to a rocky bluff with weathered lodgepole pines and hemlocks, with views of both Nanaimo and, in the opposite direction, the summit. Since there are several small trails along the bluffs, make sure you follow the red markers to avoid the cliffs. The trail drops into the forest and comes to a T-junction with a small signposted map. The broad track to the right makes a large outward sweep as an alternative downhill route.

8. The broad track leads uphill before swinging to the right. You will see a small trail leading straight upward, marked with yellow ribbon. This alternative route leads up to the gap between the two summits and allows a comparatively unexposed approach to the back of the popular western summit as well as a gravel track circling around to the eastern summit. The most popular route, though, for those who are happy with a little light scrambling, ignores this trail and carries on straight ahead.

9. The track runs parallel to the main ridge of the mountain, taking you up a fairly steep, forested section to the end of the rocky spine. Climb the rocky natural steps along the ridge to the open crest of the mountain. If you arrive in spring you will find beds of camas lilies. Later in the summer, stonecrop and harebells dot the crest.

10. You will probably want to stop here, since it is the more attractive summit. From this spot you can look west to Mt. de Cosmos and Mt. Moriarty as well as east over the coastal plain and islands around Nanaimo – Newcastle, Protection, Gabriola and farther south. Concrete foundations mark the site of a former fire lookout. From here you may choose to continue the short distance toward the highest point, featuring a transmitter tower, and the bluffs surrounding it. This requires dropping down to and circling around on a rough gravel track.

Options:

While you can descend exactly the way you came, you may well wish to take two options for variety.

1. When you come to Rafe's Way, don't take the small trail to the right but carry on straight downhill to the old road. Turn right and follow it back to the signposted main junction.

2. When you come to the large handmade sign saying "Way Down" and pointing both right and left, head left. This trail is more eroded than the other one and has some fairly slippery sections of bare dirt. In spring and early summer it leads past a little stream and a pretty waterfall in a fern-lined gorge. The trail swings away from the gorge, crosses a little streambed and rejoins the gorge just before coming out on the lakeside trail. Turn right to reach the floating bridge across the lake.

The new floating bridge over Witchcraft Lake cuts off the first part of the trail around the end of the lake (1)

This view to the southeast can be seen only by walking from the first summit to the viewpoint by the transmitter towers (8)

16. *Top Bridge and Englishman River*

14.5 km return
Start height: 21 m
Height gain: negligible
Easy
All season (trail is muddy in winter and subject to occasional flooding)

Start: From Highway 19A southeast of Parksville and the "orange bridge," turn onto Tuan Road at traffic lights, then go immediately right. A large sign for "Top Bridge Regional Trail" and a parking area are on your left.

Difficulty: From the start to the Top Bridge suspension bridge, the trail is generally broad and level, with only a few muddy spots in winter. South of the suspension bridge most of the trails next to the river are user-made and therefore uneven and winding, but still safe. At a few points they join a service road for the salmon enhancement works.

Mountain views, fern-covered cliffs, a suspension bridge by deep swimming holes and spectacular rock formations, and a long meandering trail through large firs and maples. An optional side route past spawning channels with virtually guaranteed sighting of salmon in the fall. (Don't confuse this route with Englishman River Falls Park, a provincial park in Errington with only a short trail system.)

1. The first part of the trail runs through private property but is designated park trail, well marked with blue and white signs on posts. Ignore the many side trails, though you will see plenty of local dog walkers using them. As the trail swings left it descends to join a broader track. Turn right and follow this path through small alders until it goes up a slope and enters a predominantly fir forest. The trail approaches the river and goes under a trestle and Highway 19, the Inland Island Highway.

2. The next section is probably the most scenic part of the entire trail. While side tracks lead off left to a mountain-bike park and right to the riverbank, the main route, well signposted, runs more or less directly ahead. Soon you will come to several sets of wooden stairs and a well-engineered trail below cliffs overhung with licorice ferns. You may wish to take short detours down to the riverbank to view the sculpted rock formations and deep pools or join the locals for a swim.

3. The trail emerges at a parking area. Cross the suspension footbridge. If the weather is good, pause here to watch local youth jumping from the precipitous rocks into the deep pools. A large sign identifies the next section as "Englishman River Regional Park." Ignore a user-made path a little above the riverbank and a new, well-built park trail heading uphill. This new route is most useful during flood conditions or to give variety. Virtually all locals, however, walk (or mountain bike) along the user-made riverside trails starting immediately after you cross the bridge. About 100 m along, the way crosses a rough rock section and forks again. Take the left fork across a sturdy little wooden bridge.

4. The trail next runs roughly parallel to the river, though not always right beside it. Ignore two cross-tracks, the first leading to the right across a metal bridge to a gravel road, the second a similar distance along. After swinging inland for some distance, the trail dips toward and away from the river before joining a gravel service road. Here you will find a bench with a good view of the river, and large park signs with maps and information on salmon spawning.

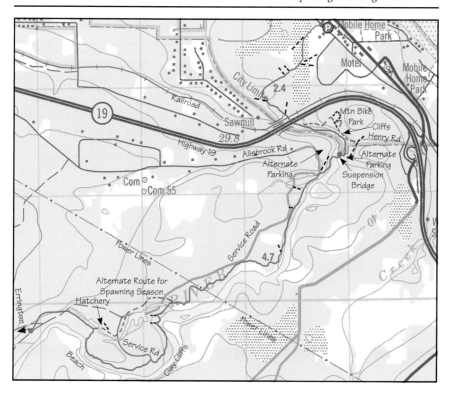

Mt. Arrowsmith from near the beginning of the trail on Industrial Way (1)

5. Rejoin the trail just behind the sign. After running along the very edge of an eroded bank, the route swings inland and emerges under power lines. Here a blue and white arrow on a post points to the right, and another a short distance farther points left to a trail entering the forest. Soon the path joins the river and then comes to a small stream with a narrow plank bridge. Cross to the left over this bridge and follow a loose, gravelly trail along a flood plain. At first it weaves through a stand of alder, passing two trails heading off to the right. Then it swings toward the rocky riverbank and follows it at river level until ending at a beach-like area opposite high clay cliffs.

6. Turn right, away from the water, on a road-width track, and within a few paces turn left, leaving this broad path to start a trail along the riverbank. As the river curves to the right for some distance you will see two broad tracks leading to the nearby bank. The second of these leads to a popular swimming spot. To get to a lovely beach clearly visible across the river, wade across the shallows at the north end of the pool.

7. From here the road-width trail leads away from the river to salmon enhancement buildings and signs. Turn left and follow a small service road parallel to spawning channels to reach the end of the route, a bench and a beautiful deep pool with the intake pipe for the spawning channels.

8. Return the way you came or take one or more of the following options.

Options

1. From the end of October to the beginning of December, you are almost guaranteed to see spawning up close. On your return, instead of turning right at the service road, go straight ahead. Once across the bridge, turn right to follow the small spawning stream, the best spot to view salmon. Cross a service road and carry on beside the stream as it leads to a "beaver pond." After leaving the beaver pond, the trail comes out on the service road. Turn right and at the first track to the right, turn right. You will see this path heading across a streambed. Find a fairly small but well-used trail heading left before the streambed. In a very short distance you will rejoin the outward-bound route at the junction with the plank bridge.

2. For a scenic loop on your way back, cross the large suspension bridge and carry on through the parking lot and uphill. Ignore trails leading off to the left. Near the top of the hill you will see a network of mountain-biking trails on your left. Turn left and head to a clifftop path. Equipped with chain-link safety fencing at the most exposed sections, the cliff-edge trail gives impressive views over the suspension bridge and the river. Just before this path starts to drop steeply, take the main trail, turning sharply right. Switchback down a fairly steep slope, turn left at a fork, and at the bottom of the hill turn left again to rejoin the signposted through trail near the river. Turn right to retrace your route.

3. To go farther up the river, take the broad, steep (signposted) track uphill from shortly before the route's southern end, described above. Take the first small trail to the left off this track and continue to take left branches. The way rises and falls fairly close to the river for well over an additional kilometre, crossing two single-rail bridges en route to a lovely beach-like area with a good swimming spot. The trail is quite rough and root-bound in some spots, and in one section it is subject to being overgrown with thimbleberries. On the whole, though, the through trail is distinct and reasonably well travelled. Road access and parking are close to this swimming/picnic area via Englishman River Road.

The most popular swimming spot is next to the suspension bridge (3)

The suspension bridge runs directly by the most popular swimming spot close to two alternate parking areas (3)

17. Mount Horne

12 km return
High point: 910 m
Height gain: ~725 m
Moderate / strenuous
April to November (depending on
   snowcover)

Giant old-growth forest followed by a varied route to mossy bluffs with excellent views of Cameron Lake, Wesley Ridge, Mt. Arrowsmith, Mt. Klitsa and the whole Alberni Valley.

Start: Cathedral Grove, the starting point of this hike, is located on Highway 4 about 500 m east of Cameron Lake. Park at Cathedral Grove and enter the MacMillan Provincial Park trails on the north side of the road (right-hand side if you're driving toward Port Alberni).

Difficulty: The trail varies considerably. Currently it is popular mostly with hiking clubs and locals, though word of its attractions is spreading quickly. The path along a dirt slope just below and above railway tracks is subject to erosion. While not dangerous, the loose dirt can be slippery without well-treaded boots. Most of the user-made trail is clear and signposted/flagged. The section along the old logging road is easy. The flagged route to the summit requires keeping alert to the route. A little scrambling is necessary at some points, but there are no exposed or dangerous drops. Some people use the trail year round, since the avalanche danger in winter is low.

1. Begin walking the trail in a clockwise direction (unless you wish to start with a circuit of the giant firs and cedars). Once you've reached the far side of the circular route you will see a short, user-made trail leading to a gravel road (Chalet Road). Walk along Chalet Road about 350 m until you pass the first two lakefront cottages. You will see a large log that has been chain-sawed to allow clear passage to the beginning of the uphill trail. There may or may not be flagging tape and a sign here, depending on the year.

2. Ascend a steep dirt and gravel slope to the old rail lines. Once you reach the

railway tracks, turn right. After about 250 m you will see a rough gravel track angling up the dirt bank and a length of thick, faded blue rope (helpful, but not really necessary). This dirt trail begins steeply and then levels slightly. Partway to the saddle between Mt. Horne and Wesley Ridge, the trail enters a particularly attractive forest of ferns and large firs and, at the saddle, intersects with the track coming from Wesley Ridge (running along the north shore of Cameron Lake).

3. Turn left and begin the climb with a few short steep sections on a largely dirt and root trail. The gradually levelling track emerges onto a gravel logging road. Turn left and begin winding up this road. Pause to enjoy the viewpoints down to Cameron Lake and, in season, feast on wild strawberries. At the midpoint of the second major leftward curve, look for a cluster of multicoloured flagging tape. The trail can be overgrown at this point, but after a minute or so it opens out.

4. From here to the summit the route is well flagged. It leads over several rocky outcroppings requiring a little scrambling and the odd handhold. It is over these outcroppings that the way is less clear, so look ahead to the next piece of flagging tape.

5. The summit has an open area with a stone cairn and sign-in booklet. The views begin with Wesley Ridge and extend down and beyond Cameron Lake to Mt. Benson and across the valley to Mt. Cokely and Mt. Arrowsmith. Looking down the Alberni Valley you will see the town of Port Alberni and Alberni Inlet leading to

Mt. Klitsa at the head of Sproat Lake is a challenging but spectacular day hike no longer with good road access (5)

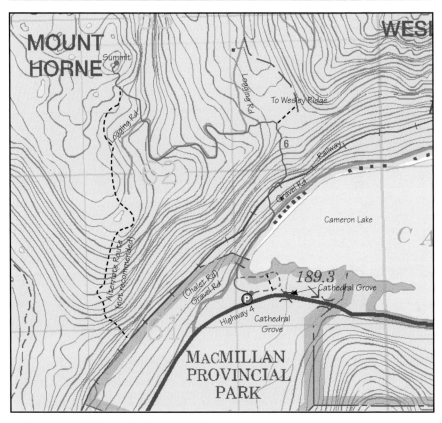

Barkley Sound. The strip of water to the right of the city is Sproat Lake, with (for valley residents) the iconic Mt. Klitsa at its end. Beyond are the spectacular peaks in Strathcona Provincial Park. If you wander amongst the pine trees along the north edge of the clearing you can get glimpses of the east coast of the Island and Hornby Island.

6. Return the way you came.

Option:

It is possible to go back down by a different, newer, flagged trail to the right (as you descend) of your original ascent route, but it is recommended that you use the more established trail you came up by, partly because it is more gradual overall and so you can avoid a long walk along railway tracks. Local outdoors enthusiasts in 2013 created a new trail starting southwest of Cathedral Grove on Highway 4. It had the great advantage of running through a large section of beautiful old forest. Unfortunately, much of this forest was destroyed by logging operations shortly thereafter.

The gravel road approach between Cathedral Grove and the trailhead gives beautiful views of Cameron Lake (1)

A panoramic view over the Alberni Valley from the rounded top of the mountain (4)

77

18. Mount Cokely

10 km for basic loop, with longer
  option
High point: 1099 m
Height gain: 915 m
Strenuous
May to October (depending on
  snowfall)

*A historic trail, now with a loop
route passing an abandoned
ski slope. Optional ascent to
Mt. Cokely summit, a spur of
the Mt. Arrowsmith massif.*

Start: On Highway 4 between Parksville and Port Alberni, at the southeast end of Cameron Lake, opposite MacMillan Provincial Park, park on a broad shoulder next to a dirt road leading into the forest.

Difficulty: The trail to the lookout – the most popular part of the route – is carefully engineered, graded with mostly smooth-surfaced dirt and switchbacked to keep slopes gradual. From the lookout to the abandoned ski lift the new trail is narrow and a little overgrown but generally easy and well marked. The historic CPR trail from the junction with the lookout trail to the old ski lifts is mostly smooth and easy, but there are some muddy patches, deadfall and small stream crossings. The top section is narrow and root-covered but clear. The upper trailheads of both tracks from the ski lodge road are a little difficult to find, though marked with flagging tape. Some climb the trail in winter and early spring, using snowshoes.

Warning:

In summer 2012, signs were posted restricting the upper parts of the trail to weekend use because of weekday blasting. Before planning a mid-week trip past the lookout, check with the Regional District of Nanaimo.

1. Follow the broad dirt road as it slants gradually away from the highway and heads gently uphill. Ignore a smaller branch to the right and, just before the actual trailhead, one to the left as well.

The small green and white trailhead sign is a little tricky to spot but the trailhead itself is obvious.

2. The route approaches McBey Creek and, via some switchbacks, gradually rises above the rushing creek at the bottom of a steep ravine. You will come to a fork with a sign warning you about the erosion of the old trail and pointing you to the right, up a new trail. In fact the old trail is not dangerously eroded at the moment, and in any case the two trails rejoin after a short distance. This section ends with a solidly built bridge overlooking a spectacular set of falls which for many walkers is their destination and turnaround point.

3. Cross the bridge and begin a long segment of gradually rising switchbacks up a steep, forested bank. The trail from the bridge to the major split is particularly well maintained. Bunchberries, maidenhair ferns and deer ferns are common along here. Occasionally you will get views out through the trees of the sharply rising bluffs to the northwest and the coastal plain.

4. At the well-signposted junction, take the left fork and continue to ascend a steep, forested bank by means of well graded switchbacks. Obviously, the loop can be walked in either direction, but by taking the left fork and doing the route clockwise, you gain altitude more quickly and have the option of making the lookout bluff your goal. In fact, when you come to a junction you will see that the branch going left to the lookout is more heavily used than the loop trail. A few minutes along

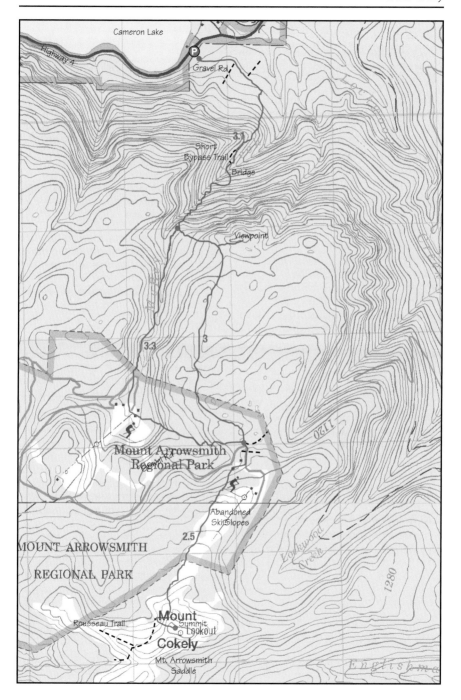

the lookout route you will rise to a rocky bluff dotted with lodgepole pines. The views over the Strait of Georgia and the Coast Mountains make this a worthwhile destination.

5. For the loop, retrace the short distance back to the junction and turn left. The trail from here to the top of the loop is easy and clear, mostly through lightly scattered forest. Bushes (mostly copperbush) are currently crowding the comparatively narrow path. After a long section of gradual ascent, the track is interrupted by a new logging road.

6. You have several options here, including crossing the logging road and picking up the last bit of trail. If your primary goal is to find the trailhead for the CPR route so you can loop back, then turn sharply right just before the logging road, down a sketchy but newly flagged track. After a short walk you will find yourself on a broad gravel road, formerly the ski resort route. Turn right.

7. Walk 200 or 300 m, scanning the right side of the road for a rough gravel track and several pieces of red flagging tape. Walk past a campfire pit and look downhill to the left, where you will see more trail markers. Once you get past this uncertain spot, the trail, though narrow, is clear and well marked. It runs more or less parallel to McBey Creek through some lovely old forest. (Try to keep your eyes averted from a patch of fresh clear-cut.)

8. Once you get to the beginning of the loop, turn left to return the way you came.

Options:

You can make a straightforward but little-used ascent of Mt. Cokely (1619 m) from the old ski resort located more or less between the two trailheads. This involves ascending about 500 m. Until midsummer, the upper part is often dotted with snow patches and awash with melting snow. A little light scrambling is necessary just below the summit.

Most ascents of Mt. Cokely take the Mt. Arrowsmith Saddle route (see Hike 19). Those who climb it from the old ski lodge sometimes drive to this spot rather than hike from Cameron Lake.

1. As you emerge from the lookout trail, turn left instead of right and ascend the gravel road a short distance until you come to a large former parking area. From here you will see a rough gravel track (much abused by quads) leading straight up a former ski run.

2. At the end of this track pick up a route indicated by red flagging tape and fluorescent red paint sprayed on rock outcroppings. You will see few other signs of a trail, but the route is fairly obvious up the low, irregular ridgeline.

3. When you get to a gully cutting across in front of you, cross at the high point. The paint tracks – sometimes a little hard to spot – lead you straight toward the summit (marked with a transmitter and small building). As you approach the ramparts below the summit, swing right to gain the ridge leading to the summit. If you arrive when there is still snow, you will need to take care if the snow is icy. Consider turning back. Although there is little exposure, sliding out of control down the snow could cause injury.

4. Return the way you came.

The summit of Mt. Cokely with the relay tower (O3)

Sproat Lake and Mt. Klitsa seen from throughout the Alberni Valley (O2)

81

The upstream falls from the bridge over McBey Creek (2)

19. *Mount Arrowsmith Saddle Route*

3.6 km return (plus two options)
High point: 1582 m
Height gain: 544 m
Moderate
June to October (expect some
snowfields in June)

Difficulty: Although the first part of the route, to the saddle, is fairly steep and physically demanding, it is comparatively short. Careful footing is required at only a few points. From the saddle to the Cokely ridge involves scrambling and care but no real danger. The optional return route – Rousseau Ridge Trail along the Cokely ridge – is uneven but not steep except in one short section. Because avalanche danger is fairly low (though not zero), this route can be hiked year round with proper equipment and safety precautions.

Start: Just past the highest point of Highway 4, marked with a summit sign, en route to Port Alberni, turn left onto a gravel road where you see a large sign saying "Arrowsmith Ski Area." After 2.7 km on a fairly rough gravel road, descend to a T-junction. Turn left on this broad gravel logging road (called Cameron Main). In just under 8 km you will see a fork turning uphill on the left and a wooden sign saying "Mt. Arrowsmith." After ascending over a rough but passable road, count the four hairpin turns. When you reach a sharp turn left after a period of contouring ascent, 7 km from the junction, park on a broad gravel shoulder. (You will be able to see the saddle from here.)

No other trail on Vancouver Island allows you to get up to the subalpine so easily and quickly. Wonderful wildflower displays in mid- to late summer (after snow melt); great views of the Arrowsmith "humps," the Alberni Valley and peaks and the east coast of the Island. Probably the most popular ascent of a "proper mountain" on the island.

1. Just to the right of a small stream, head up an old roadbed through a former clearcut, now covered with small trees. Where the road starts to curve sharply left you will see a similar track heading more or less straight ahead.

2. Take this flagged route to the edge of the forest. From here the trail, maintained and repaired by volunteers, switchbacks fairly steeply through trees. Ignore a small path heading left toward a stream. Although the trail to the saddle is generally clear and obvious, with occasional pieces of flagging tape, be careful not to lose your way when you come to small bluffs of exposed rock. Make sure you are on a clear, flagged path after crossing these bluffs, since some false trails have been created by hikers wandering off the main route.

3. As you leave the forest, climbing over an increasing number of patches of bare rock (one of them with a helpful but unnecessary piece of rope), the path becomes generally less steep until you arrive at the base of the scree slope 200 m before the saddle.

4. Avoid the temptation to drop down into the scree, though you will see evidence of others having done that. Keep well up to the left along the trail, which is sometimes faint. This is an area that can be particularly rich in wildflowers, especially columbines and yellow avalanche lilies, in mid- to late summer, depending on when the snow melts.

5. The saddle is a perfect place to wander, rest and picnic. Even if you want to proceed directly to the loop route, take at least a small detour to your right so you can get

Beautiful Jewel Lake is mostly surrounded by steep cliffs, but can be reached by descending from the central part of the saddle (5)

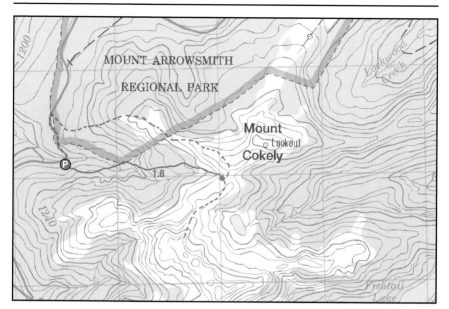

a view of Jewel Lake, in a bowl beneath a spectacular series of cliffs and peaks. In addition, though you may wish to return the way you came, consider scrambling up the ridge to your left (toward Mt. Cokely) for views across the coastal plain.

6. Return the way you came.

Options:

1. You can make a loop of this hike (1 km longer than the direct return) by heading left on Rousseau Ridge Trail along the Mt. Cokely ridge. From the high point, follow the gradually descending ridge. Make sure you stick to the flagged route along the ridgetop. Avoid the temptation to shortcut left down to the trailhead: you will encounter several areas of cliffs. After the ridge drops significantly and starts to rise again, follow the flagged route back toward the ridgeline, making sure you maintain elevation on the left fork of the Y-shaped end of the ridge. The last part of the trail leads more or less off the left end of the ridge. Again, stick to the marked route, at one point dropping over some fairly steep rock and down a sharply descending gully. The last part of the descent is in trees. When you reach the gravel road, turn left and walk back to your vehicle.

2. From the saddle you can easily climb the first two "bumps" of Mt. Arrowsmith, though a little scrambling is required. Don't attempt to go beyond the second bump (1691 m) unless you have technical skills and the proper equipment. In addition, don't climb these bumps in low visibility unless you have a compass and/or GPS. If you become disoriented you might accidently start down an apparent ridgeline that becomes dangerously steep. Add 2 km return to the saddle.

From partway to the saddle, the first of the "bumps" leading off the saddle is clearly visible. Snow can linger well into July after a particularly snowbound winter (3)

The meadows of wild flowers just before the summit are spectacular. The time of blooming varies from year to year, depending on the snow cover, but August is the best most years (4)

20. Mount Arrowsmith Judges Route

6 km return
High point: 1819 m
Height gain: 944 m
Moderately strenuous
June to October

Probably the most popular peak hike on Vancouver Island and the highest mountain south of Strathcona Park, Mt. Arrowsmith is in fact a massif of several different peaks. An easy, high-elevation start, a challenging but non-technical trail past a series of increasingly high peaks to the summit. Great views along the other peaks of the massif, the east coast of Vancouver Island, Alberni Valley and peaks of Strathcona Provincial Park.

Start: From Highway 17 a little below the summit on the Port Alberni side, you will see a large, old sign saying "Mt. Arrowsmith Ski Area." The first section of fairly rough gravel road winds for a little over 2.5 km to a junction with the much smoother Cameron Main, also gravel. Follow Cameron Main for 7.7 km. You should see an old "Mt. Arrowsmith" sign on a tree and another gravel road cutting sharply uphill to the left. Go 2.8 km, keeping alert for a very rough gravel road on your right with flagging tape and, 70 m beyond that, a pulloff area on your left. If you reach a switchback, you've gone too far.

Difficulty: This mountain can normally be climbed earlier in the year than peaks of similar height, since the snow usually disappears comparatively quickly. The first part of the trail, over packed dirt, can be slippery during dry weather. Wear shoes/boots with good grip. Be aware that a whole line of flagging tape, marking a boundary, has recently been set. Make sure you are walking on a well-beaten path and not chasing a piece of flagging tape into the woods. Above the treeline, a little scrambling over rocky outcroppings is necessary but there are no exposed drops. Avoid heavy cloud or fog: losing your way could take you to some dangerously steep sections.

1. Walk the short distance along the road back to the flagged branch road and follow it to its end.

2. The first part of the route is mostly on packed dirt under trees. Although generally clear and well flagged, this much-used trail can be lost if you are not paying attention and wander down unflagged side tracks. Partway along you will come to a pleasant rest and view spot on a small bluff of exposed rock.

3. Although there is no distinct treeline, you will fairly quickly find that the trees are noticeably thinning out. The peak to your left, though impressive-looking as you approach it, is only 1670 m.

4. By the time you have scrambled over a few areas of solid rock and a few small scree areas you will reach a col, or confined saddle between ridges. Here you will normally see the impressive remains of the previous summer's snow forming a large wedge dropping dizzily to the north side of the mountain. You can look back down onto the peak you have just passed and appreciate your ascent.

5. From the col to the summit the trail takes you a little to the right over an intervening bump and then up to the summit itself. Rather than climb straight up the rounded rock face below the summit, circle to the right around its base and make your way up a small cleft. At the summit you will see a wooden helicopter platform, one of the communications towers that dot various peaks on the island, and, at a cairn, a canister containing a little booklet in which you can record your achievement.

Nearing the col before the summit (5)

5. Return the way you came, taking care not to try a new route just because it looks easy from where you are standing. Keep to the flagged route.

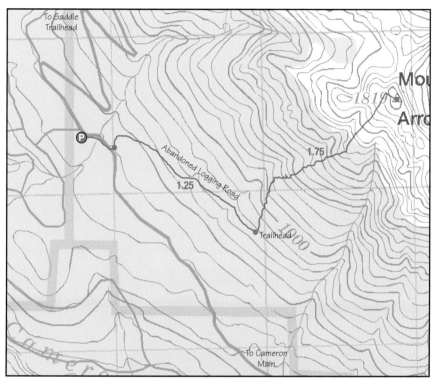

The view from the summit to four of the lower bumps, and northwest towards Denman Island (5)

Mt. Cokely and the east coast of the island with Texada Island

21. Mount Moriarty

7.5 km return
High point: 1610 m
Height gain: 694 m
Moderately strenuous
June to October

A lakeside trail leading though large trees to a gradually ascending open ridge with subalpine vegetation and views across the coastal plain and mid-island mountains. Mt. Moriarty is the highest peak south of Mt. Arrowsmith.

Start: Just past the "Summit" sign at the highest point of Highway 4 between Port Alberni and Cameron Lake, turn left onto a gravel road where you see a large sign saying "Arrowmith Ski Area." After 2.7 km on a fairly rough gravel road, you will descend to a junction with a broad gravel road (Cameron Main). Turn left on this comparatively well graded road. When you come to the signposted fork to Mt. Arrowsmith pointing to the left, start watching your odometer. Your destination is 13 km from here. Keep left when you see a sign saying "CAM 21" pointing right. Keep left again when you see "CAM 271" on your right, and keep right when you see "CAM 266" on your left. Park just below the first switchback heading left uphill. You should see a wooden sign saying "Labour Day Lake," though the trailhead may be obscured by thimbleberry bushes. Of all hikes in this book, this is the one most vulnerable to difficulties with logging road access. To improve the likelihood of a trouble-free drive to the trailhead, come on a weekend.

Difficulty: Most of the trail through the trees is clear and well flagged, though it may require climbing over occasional deadfall. Once into the subalpine, the route can be a little harder to find, especially if it crosses lingering patches of snow. Keep a sharp eye out for flagging tape and cairns, though in fact refinding a lost route is usually easy. Since there are few dangerous cliffs, the trail follows the ridgeline closely (except toward the summit). The section requiring the most scrambling occurs fairly early along the ridge. There is no significant exposure, however. In low visibility, it is important not to wander to the right (north) on snowfields, since these can be heavily corniced, hanging over steep drops.

1. The path runs basically level for about 1 km, first taking you through an open, bushy canopy and crossing several streams. Many short sections of boardwalk and small bridges help, though some have been damaged. Once you get to a camping area with a firepit, look for a huge rock beside a cluster of trees and an unsignposted path leading straight uphill.

2. From the beginning the trail is well flagged and generally narrow but clear. There may be an occasional fallen log. The route leads more or less straight uphill, then starts angling right (east). Unusually, part of the trail is in a streambed, though the woods are open enough that it is easy to walk out of the small stream gully if it is more comfortable to do so. The second half of the trail up to the ridge is less steep than the first half.

3. Once the trail hits the ridge, the view suddenly opens up, in part because the trees are smaller and sparser. After a short distance, scramble up a section of ledges and bluffs, dotted with subalpine flowers. All the way to the summit, the trail gradually ascends over rounded crests of solid rock outcroppings. There are fewer flags here, since the trees are broadly spaced, but in most cases the trail itself is well worn and marked by occasional cairns. Some steep cliffs drop from the east side of the ridge, so be careful descending if cloud settles in.

4. The fairly confined summit is marked by a tapering aluminum cairn and a register where you can record your

Snow can linger well into August (3)

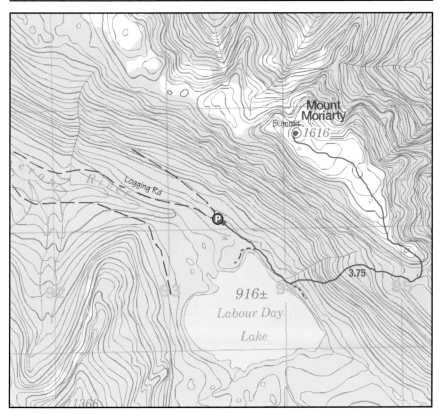

achievement. Exploring around the summit allows you some views you wouldn't otherwise have from the summit itself. Probably most striking are the panoramas of Mt. Arrowsmith along the ridges to the northwest and the whole coastal plain on the east coast of the Island. On a clear day the white cone of Mt. Baker is hauntingly clear.

5. Descend the way you came.

Options:

When you get back down to Labour Day Lake, you may wish to make a circuit of the lake on the trail, particularly popular with fishermen. The whole circuit of the lake is just under 4 km. Recently the trail has occasionally been closed because of blasting/logging road work on the south shore.

The trail along the north shore of Labour Day Lake crosses several small bridges (2)

The view to the northeast with the logging roads visible that some hardy souls use to reach the northeast face and a difficult ascent (4)

22. *Nile Creek*

14 km return
High point: 250 m
Height gain: 230 m
Easy / moderate
All season

A small, winding forest trail through large maples, firs and cedars, mostly near a splashing salmon stream. The trail ends with a sequence of several high falls twisting through a narrow gorge.

Start: From Highway 19A at 16 km north of Qualicum Beach and 40 km south of Courtenay, turn onto Charlton Drive and follow it to its end. Charlton Drive is about 200 m south of a small bridge (over Nile Creek, but not signposted).

Difficulty: The trail is generally easy and clear, but in wet weather some of the logs laid over muddy sections can become slippery. Some sections, especially west of Highway 19, require being reasonably sure-footed. Because the trail is not part of a park system, and is currently popular mostly with locals, some parts of it can become a little overgrown with salmonberry and thimbleberry, particularly to the north of Highway 19.

1. Head past a red gate along a gravel road, passing under a railway trestle. You will see Nile Creek on your right. You will also pass a sturdy footbridge that crosses the creek and on your left a boardwalk leading into the forest. Both of these are part of the Lighthouse Country Regional Trail system. Ignore both. Another 100 m along this gravel road you will see worksheds (and an interesting carving) belonging to the Nile Creek Enhancement Society.

2. When you come to the end of the narrow gravel road running parallel to the creek, carry on straight ahead along a broad, even path under large maples, grand firs and hemlocks. After a short distance, the trail crosses the creek by means of a large tree trunk with a handrail.

3. After leaving and rejoining the creek, ignore a trail to the left crossing a log bridge. When you come to a small, hand-lettered sign indicating an "alternate trail" to the right and the more scenic "river trail" to the left, you can take either one, since they rejoin a little farther on. Later ignore a mountain-biking trail on the right. Carry on straight ahead.

4. Just under 3 km from your starting point, the path enters a clear area, well above the creek, and passes under Highway 19. For the next section, the trail is somewhat rougher and more irregular. It runs largely away from the creek and under comparatively small trees. Be prepared to walk along several logs and rough boardwalks.

5. The route rejoins the creek at a particularly impressive pair of large trees, one cedar, the other Douglas fir. The next section is probably the narrowest and roughest part of the trail, though considerable work has been done in the form of rough board crossings of muddy sections and rope hand-assists for walking along fallen logs.

6. When you reach the first set of falls, comparatively small but nevertheless beautiful, you will find that the trail generally improves. As you climb this last part you will pass a sequence of falls, the highest dropping more than 15 m. This final section of trail to a logging road crossing is particularly broad and well engineered with steps and supports because it is frequently used by those using 4x4s to approach the falls from the logging roads above the falls. Through this section the track climbs significantly. Above the falls it rises steeply through a fairly open, rocky

A handrail and level surface make this picturesque log crossing to the north shore of Nile Creek easy (2)

section before descending via a set of dirt and board steps to a flat, open area beside a slow-moving part of the creek. This makes a good picnic spot and turnaround.

7. If you wish to view one more set of scenic falls, carry on up the fairly steep but well-maintained trail to a washed-out logging road. If the creek is low and the water not too cold, you may choose to cross the creek and make your way a little under 100 m around the logging roads away from and back towards the creek. Climb over the mossy rock above the falls for the best view of these cascades. Otherwise, instead of crossing the creek, carry on for 50 m up the logging road and turn left to climb over an area of bare, mossy rocks and a lovely, though restricted, view of the top falls.

8. Return the way you came.

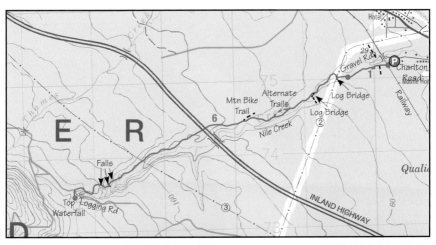

The first and smallest of the sequence of falls (6)

One of the highest of the sequence of falls near the west end of the trail (6)

23. *Puntledge River East*

8.6 km return
High point: 134 m
Height gain: 20 m
Easy
All season

A well-maintained, level, forested path close to the banks of a very slow (dammed) river with amazingly clear water.

Start: Turn off Highway 19 at the southern exit to Courtenay on the Comox Valley Parkway, and after 2 km turn onto Cumberland Road for 300 m. Turn left onto Marsden Road for 2.3 km, then left onto Lake Trail Road for 3.6 km. Look for a yellow metal barred gate at the entrance to a gravel road just before the Comox Lake Hostel (called Bevan Hostel on some signs).

Difficulty: The path is smooth and largely level. Bridges and boardwalks cross its wet areas. Footpaths intersect with horse and mountain-biking routes.

1. Pass through the gate and walk straight ahead through the bushy cleared area. Cross a gravel track, past some signs, and carry on ahead until you reach the riverside and a clearing with an outhouse. You will see a sign for "Bevan Hostel" pointing back the way you came. (Those interested in such things may wish to make a 200 m detour along the river path to the right to view the dam where the huge pipe for Courtenay's water supply begins. The dam is heavily fenced and not open to the public. Don't expect to be able to cross the river here if you hope to make a circular walk up the north bank of the river and back along the south. Return along the river trail to your previous spot.)

2. Follow the riverside trail past a broad, almost lake-like section of the river till you come to a puzzling signpost with the words "Most Difficult," apparently pointing along the river trail (and "Bevan Trail" slightly to the left). This actually points to a "difficult" cycle track leading slightly inland, not the riverside trail.

Cross "Greg's Bridge" and carry on by the river.

3. Later you will pass another signpost with two branching trails intended for mountain bikers. Keep on by the river. Within a short distance you will reach a good viewpoint with a log bench and a wooden bridge with handrails. "Palm Beach" is the name given to a small bit of sloping shore 200 m along where a horse trail comes close to the riverside path.

4. Along the last section of the trail you can take a short detour to a signposted viewpoint. The route crosses a boardwalk through a marshy area but otherwise follows the river's edge more or less all the way to an area of various converging trails and tracks with a dizzying series of signposts. Since you can see the dam and the end of the trail from here, simply make your way past the heavily fenced upper dam.

5. Cross the bridge and enter a wide riverside meadow with picnic benches and outhouse. This is a good rest spot and turnaround. The gravel road that crosses the bridge here is a continuation of Lake Trail Road, on which you parked to begin your walk. Those wanting to walk the trail in only one direction can arrange a pickup here. Note that this is also the starting point for the much longer Hike 24, "Comox Lake to Nymph Falls."

6. For the most attractive return route, go back the way you came.

Option:

If you wish cut about 1.5 km off your return trip but still walk largely through forest (and away from the river), follow the signs for "Bevan Trail" all the way back to the service road by which you first came to the river. Note that this is a "multi-use" trail, so you may encounter mountain bikers or horses. Also note that when you see signs pointing, confusingly, to "Bevan Hostel," these are not actually pointing directly to the hostel (near your car), but merely to the shortest route to the service road by the hostel. On posted maps along the trail, the hostel (and your starting point) is, again confusingly, called "Comox Lake Hostel." Be prepared for some slightly disorienting arrays of signs where biking trails leave and rejoin "Bevan Trail."

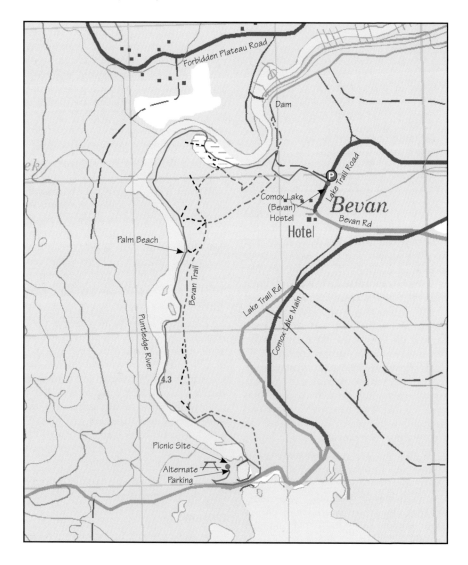

The picnic ground almost immediately across the bridge at the west end of the trail is also accessible by road (5)

About a kilometre along the trail, a bend in the river forms a large lagoon-like pool, a favourite spot for water fowl and, here, a trumpeter swan

Cedars, generally light green, line the river bank and stand out against the darker firs

24. Comox Lake to Nymph Falls

14.5 km return via two small loops
High point: 138 m
Height gain on return: 55 m
Easy (but quite long)
All season

A forested walk along a nearly level trail, first alongside the mirror-calm Puntledge River and later, after a dam and salmon hatchery, to a fast-flowing and dramatic series of rapids called Nymph Falls.

Start: Turn off Highway 19 at the exit for Courtenay south, and after 2.2 km on the Comox Valley Parkway, turn left onto Cumberland Road for 300 m. Turn left onto Marsden Road for 2.3 km, then left onto Lake Trail Road for 2.5 km. Make a left onto Comox Lake Road and continue as it crosses Bevan Road and becomes Comox Logging Road (unsignposted) until, 2.4 km after Bevan Road, you cross a bridge with a dam. Just across, you will come to the signposted entrance to a parking lot and a park with picnic benches. The road into the park is sometimes gated well into spring, so you may have to park along the side of the road and walk the 100 m into the park and the beginning of the trail.

Difficulty: This is a broad, well-built trail, generally smooth and surfaced with crushed gravel. It is well signposted and mostly clear of mud even during winter months. Bridges take you across small tributaries of the Puntledge River. You will encounter few changes of elevation and only near the northeast end.

1. Ignore the imposing gateway for "Bear Bait Trail" leading from the grassy picnic area. This is a cycling trail, named by someone with a grim sense of humour. Take the trail to the right of this sign and after a few metres you will see a post with a small blue and white sign for "River Trail." This is the route you will be following all the way to Nymph Falls Regional Park. (If you are using the latest topo map, note that the park is marked inaccurately.) The first part of the trail runs fairly close to and only slightly above the river, which is almost always within view through a lattice of branches. Because it is dammed (this is the water supply for Courtenay) the river is almost as still as a lake at this stage.

2. You will pass two loop trails leading off to your left and heading back to the starting point. Keep ahead on the signposted "River Trail." Shortly after passing a small wooden 1.5 km sign high on a tree you will come to a bench and a "Bypass Trail" sign. This cuts off a loop and saves almost 1 km on your return. At this point, though, ignore the sign and carry on along River Trail. Shortly after, the trail in fact leaves the river and zigzags significantly before joining the other end of Bypass Trail.

3. For the next section, you are away from the river, crossing several small tributaries while walking through an area that was logged off fairly recently. On this nearly road-width stretch, walkers share the trail with cyclists.

4. Immediately after crossing a bridge the trail splits. At this junction you will notice a broad track leading to a distant paved road. This is Forbidden Plateau Road, heading up the mountain and connecting with the Nymph Falls Regional Park trailhead. Turn right, onto the signposted River Trail running alongside a pretty stream. Shortly after you rejoin the main river, a broad track leads to the riverbank, where gravel has been dumped to improve spawning conditions for salmon.

5. The next section takes you well above the river, past a salmon hatchery to a roadway and large fenced-off area surrounding the lower dam. For about 500 m you will be sharing the way with cyclists riding Bear Bait Trail.

6. Turning again onto the River Trail you will pass high above a striking twist in the river. Some 400 m from the dam, watch for an unsignposted and somewhat rough side path leading to a spectacular fenced clifftop viewing spot. Shortly after this viewpoint there is another, equally good one.

7. You will soon come to the boundary of Nymph Falls Park and a clearing with an outhouse and a side track to Forbidden Plateau Road. The park is full of a network of intersecting trails, many of them used by mountain bikers. Keep to the riverside path. When you come to an open picnic area, you may wish to pause to eat your sandwiches, since there are no picnic tables next to the falls. Otherwise, you will soon begin the section of trail alongside the increasingly steep rapids that make up Nymph Falls.

8. Carry on past the falls to begin the loop trail that makes a good turnaround end to the outward leg of the hike. Walk this 1.3 km loop counterclockwise by following the signs that lead you first along the river and then through the forest and back to the river near the falls.

9. If you have arranged a one-way shuttle, you would now head back to the parking area. Otherwise, return the way you came. You may wish to shorten this route by almost 1 km by taking the signposted "Bypass Trail" on the return route.

One of two adjoining viewpoints near the southern end of Nymph Falls Park (6)

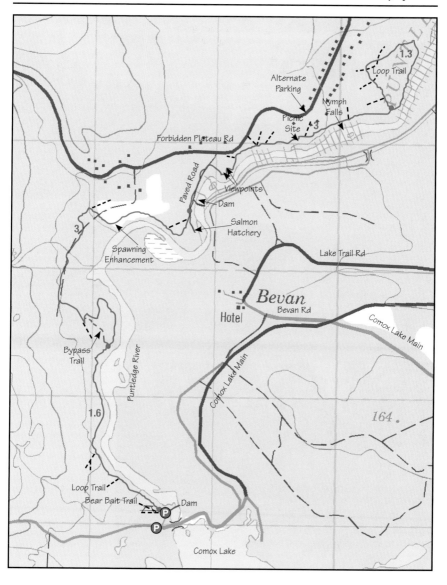

A sandstone promontory into the river mid-falls gives a great viewpoint onto the falls (7)

Nymph Falls is particularly impressive in spring

25. Mount Becher

11 km return (longer loop option)
High point: 1390 m
Height gain: 490 m
Moderate
June to October

Skeletal remains of an abandoned ski resort, great views across the Strait of Georgia, then of Comox Glacier and Mt. Albert Edward. Subalpine meadows, knolls and tarns.

Start: From Highway 19 northwest of Courtenay, at the Piercy Road exit, drive to Forbidden Plateau Road. Turn right and follow the road to its end several kilometres later. It will first cross Highway 19 via an overpass and then begin winding uphill through several switchbacks. The last few kilometres are well graded gravel. Park in the large parking area by the burnt-out remains of a former ski lodge at about 780 m elevation.

Difficulty: The initial difficulty is due to encroaching vegetation on the formerly broad tracks, also now increasingly rutted. Once the trail crosses the park boundary, though, it is smooth sailing except for the occasional wet spot or lingering snow patch. Although the path to the summit is generally clear, it is faint over some stretches of bare rock. In any case, because the mountain is so rounded, many routes are possible. Because the ascent is so gradual, this is a favourite route for backcountry skiers and snowshoers.

1. The first part of the trail, up the former downhill ski run, has several options, often criss-crossing. While this part of the route has the least pleasant walking, in large part because of encroaching bushes, it compensates with wonderful views over Courtenay and across the Strait of Georgia to the Coast Range. The easiest route begins behind the chalet ruins. Go straight uphill on a rutted roadbed and at a junction turn left.

2. Bushy at the beginning, the road opens again and goes left under the chairlift before swinging back to the right (northwest) of the chairlift. Ignore the narrow track on your left going straight uphill and carry on away from the chairlift. Note an overgrown track coming in from your left, since you will want to ignore it on your way back. Again when you reach the top of the steep uphill section, another track feeds in from the left that you will want to ignore on the return.

3. The trail enters the forest, passes a small lake on the left, then the ruins of a T-bar station on your right. Fork left slightly at the next intersection and after a slight rise you will see a track cutting in from the left and, high on a tree, a sign indicating this to be the boundary of Strathcona Provincial Park. Go straight ahead to the posted map for the park. A little later you will see several signs indicating destinations on the route.

4. At an unsignposted split in the trail a short distance along, swing right. From there to the summit the path is generally broad and clear, with a few patches of mild scrambling over rocky outcroppings. The track gradually drops through fairly thick forest and then begins the gradual ascent along the increasingly rocky and exposed flank of the mountain. You will see old, hand-carved signs pointing a side route to Boston Lake (a difficult descent) and later, just after passing a little lake, "To the Top."

5. A few cairns dot the gradual ascent but it is possible to choose several different routes to avoid lingering patches of snow. Although the summit is bordered by an area of large cliffs dropping to Boston Lake, the mountaintop is broad.

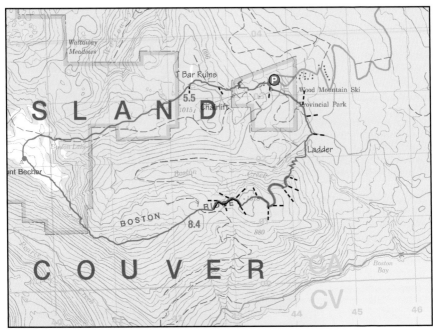

The first, bushy part of the hike is under abandoned ski lifts. Continuous views across and along the Island's east coast, here southeast across Denman and Hornby islands, Mt. Benson (Hike 15) visible as a distinct little cone (1)

6. Return the way you came (by far the most popular option).

Option:

You can choose to return via a circle route over Boston Ridge. On your way to the summit, you can see Boston Ridge converging from your left. The first crest of the ridge is visible to the east from the summit of Mt. Becher. This return track was never as popular as the main route, because it is considerably more demanding. That and the fact that clear-cut logging devastated part of the lower ridge meant the path became little used. A group of volunteers, though, has recently made a mammoth effort to clear and mark a way through the destroyed area, so it is showing every sign of becoming much more popular.

If you are prepared for the greater distance (8.4 km instead of 5.5), plus an extra 250 m of uphill climbing and some fairly steep sections, you will be well rewarded with a trail that has much more sustained time with spectacular views than the main route. In addition, the path itself can be seen as a bit of an adventure in navigating varied terrain.

1. Since the rounded summit area can be disorienting with its criss-crossing tracks, glance at your compass, head south-south-east and you will very quickly spot cairns, a trail and orange marking tape. The whole first long section of Boston Ridge is regularly marked and fairly easy to find, in part because it follows the ridgeline. Wonderful views over Comox Glacier, Comox Lake and Cruikshank Canyon open up.

2. The descent into a trough cutting across the ridge is fairly steep and requires a little careful footing. This low part of the ridge and the ascent from it are at present quite brushy with black huckleberries and copperbush. Once you reach the top of the bump the trail is much clearer again and the views open up. The descent to the next low point is straightforward but sometimes a little faint. You will soon reach the clear-cut.

3. The sequence through the clear-cut chaos seems much longer than it actually is. The recent flagging, spray painting and handmade yellow signs help enormously and the slash-clearing makes the walking easy. From the first gravel road, go downhill to a T-junction and turn left, then go to the next T-junction and turn right. At the next junction, turn left and follow the road curving to the right until a cairn and spray paint on your left direct you onto a lovely section of the original trail through forest up and over a crest.

4. Emerging downhill onto a road, turn right and follow the road in a double S-curve, ignoring both a road to the right and then a fork to the left. The tags and signs on trees along the right-hand side of the road don't indicate trails into the woods but are there to reassure you. As the road curves right, you'll see a cairn on the left indicating another short section of the old trail over a wooded crest.

5. After a short distance in the woods the route emerges into a tangled mess of recent slash, through which, though, a clear, easy way has been opened up. On the next road, take a sharp left and follow the curve to the right until a cairn and flagging tape indicate the beginning of another cleared route through the last section of slash.

6. Enter the forest onto an attractive section of old trail that soon descends steeply down a rooty bank. As you approach a splashing little stream, ignore a level track to the right. Follow the main route left to the stream, cross over a logjam and climb up a ladder and rope-assisted bit of trail which, after a short distance, comes to another small stream.

7. Take the track into some alders on the right and begin a sequence of old roadbeds that ascends about 100 vertical metres to your starting point. Since you'll soon be on a downhill mountain-bike route, tire tracks will mark the fairly obvious way.

One of many pools near the summit (5)

Cruikshank Canyon drops dramatically off the edge of the ridge (O1)

26. The Lakes of Forbidden Plateau

22.6 km loop (with shorter options)
High point: 1245 m
Height gain: 300 m (cumulative over many ups and downs)
Easy / moderate
May to November

The easiest way into the subalpine on Vancouver Island. Meadows, wildflowers, lakes, wonderful views of Mt. Albert Edward and Castlecrag Mountain.

Start: From Highway 19 northwest of Courtenay take the exit to Mt. Washington on Strathcona Parkway. As you approach Mt. Washington, take the left fork toward Raven Lodge and the Nordic Ski Centre. Signs, buildings and posted maps clearly mark the trailhead.

Difficulty: The first part of the route could hardly be easier, since it is mostly on boardwalks through Paradise Meadows. Thereafter, the trails are clear and generally easy, if occasionally a little wet, especially with lingering spring snow. All routes are well signposted. The whole area is used in winter and spring by snowshoers and backcountry skiers, since there is virtually no risk of avalanches.

While the recommended route is a kind of "grand tour" of the lakes of Forbidden Plateau, it can be cut short at many points.

1. The first part of the trail runs through the extremely popular Paradise Meadows, an oval area of ponds, streams and ground too damp for most evergreens, though there are some. Trailside signs identify many of the plant species. At a signposted junction, turn left and begin the clockwise circuit of the meadows.

2. At the next junction, turn left again and follow the gradually rising trail, no longer a boardwalk, toward Battleship Lake. As you approach the lake, take time to turn left off the main track to follow smaller paths to some excellent view spots along the lake. The route along Battleship Lake is generally close enough to the lake to give some excellent views. You will come

to another junction and series of signs, including some very old carved-wood signs pointing the way to Lake Helen Mackenzie and your next destination, Croteau Lake.

3. As you approach tiny Kooso Lake on your right you will see a small, user-made trail leading off to the meadows at the south end of the lake. Carry on straight ahead. Here, and at a few points later on, you will find the route splits and rejoins, usually because a high trail was created to avoid patches of lingering snow and/or mud. While Lady Lake, next on your right, provides pleasant views, it is Croteau Lake, farther along on your right, where you should linger. Several user-made tracks run over the low rocky headlands around this side of the lake.

4. Back on the main trail, you will come to a significant junction with a side track to the left. This side path, well-signposted, leads to the east entrance of the park off the now abandoned ski lodge on Forbidden Plateau Road (see Hike 25). Carry on to Kwai Lake, where you will see several tent sites and a high, raised outhouse. Kwai is the premier spot for taking photos of lakes and mountains, though Castlecrag and Frink are the main summits visible, since Mt. Albert Edward, the highest nearby peak, is obscured by trees.

5. Follow the sign pointing to Circlet Lake. A short distance along you will see a comparatively small path and an old wooden sign saying "Canyon and Lake Beautiful." It is 1.5 km to the end of this dead-end trail, but if you're energetic it

can provide some wonderful views. The route toward Circlet Lake rises and drops noticeably and at times is a little rough underfoot. You will come to a junction with signs pointing to Lake Helen Mackenzie and thus the recommended way back to your starting point. For the full lake tour, continue on toward Circlet Lake, dramatically situated at the base of a sequence of high cliffs. The return trip to Circlet Lake and back to this junction will add about 4.5 km to your overall trip.

6. Once on the return leg toward Lake Helen Mackenzie, you will find the trail generally easy going. Pass a sign pointing to Hairtrigger Lake, visible a short distance off the main route. From here to Lake Helen Mackenzie you will pass a few ponds on mostly gentle, meadow-like terrain before beginning the steep, heavily treed descent.

This part of the trail is a little muddy and root-bound in sections. It can also seem disproportionately long, because you don't get any good views of the largest lake on this tour until you reach the lake's north shore, several kilometres along.

From the north end of Lake Helen Mackenzie, where you will find outhouses and a large directional sign, the trail widens significantly and becomes more heavily used. As you approach Paradise Meadows, you will pass several small ponds, a lovely stream and sections of boardwalk. One final junction, shortly before the end of the route, leads leftward a few hundred metres to your starting point and rightward to the part of the Paradise Meadows circuit not on this itinerary.

Option:

If you're starting to feel tired by the time you reach Kwai Lake, you can turn to the right

The first part of the trail through Paradise Meadows is mostly on boardwalks (1)

Mt. Frink has no distinct summit from this angle. It can be easily reached by the Mt. Albert Edward approach ridge

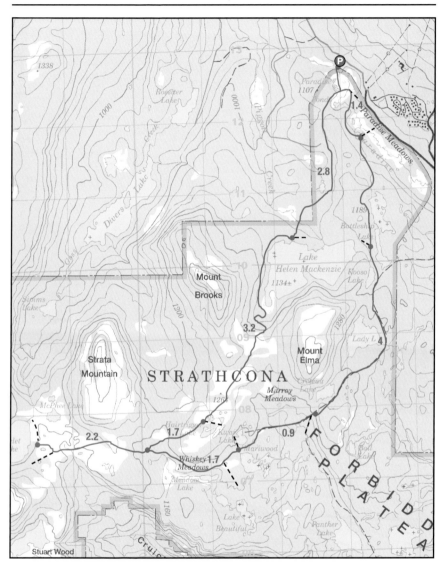

at the end of Kwai and take a shortcut to Hairtrigger Lake. By this route, 1 km later, you would join the main, western trail back to the parking lot.

If you would like to climb Mt. Albert Edward as part of a day hike, you should start and end your hike with the trail running along the left shore of Lake Helen Mackenzie. This route is somewhat shorter and much faster than the one that goes past Battleship, Lady and Kwai Lakes. Be sure to take water purifying tablets and a headlamp, since this is a very long day hike, suitable only for the very fit and the very determined.

Paradise Meadows is dotted with pretty little ponds and water lilies

27. Crest Mountain

10 km return
High point: 1566 m
Height gain: 1240 m
Strenuous
June to October

Stream crossings, large trees, subalpine flowers. Striking views of nearby peaks from a rounded, open summit dotted with picturesque tarns.

Start: From Campbell River, keep on Highway 28 across the bridge between Buttle and Upper Campbell lakes and along the Elk River. Cross the signposted bridge over the Elk and 5 km later watch for the BC Parks sign and parking lot for Crest Mountain on your right.

Difficulty: The bridge approach to the route has been recently upgraded. The path itself is clear and good, but like most mountain trails it requires climbing over rooty sections and possibly deadfall. A log bridge over a stream has a good surface and a handrail. There is no exposure and no significant scrambling. Those who are properly prepared and equipped use this trail virtually all year round because avalanche danger is low.

1. Park beside the road at a clearly marked gravel pull-off. You will see a posted map of the route, though it is a little misleading in showing the trail to be more featureless than it actually is. The trailhead is at the end of this parking lot. The broad, clear track leads a short distance to a narrow neck of water connecting the Drum Lakes. A strong bridge here has replaced an older, broken one. The trail passes an impressive bit of stream management work under some large old-growth trees.

2. A few minutes later as the route starts uphill, look for a wooden sign saying "Crest Mountain Trail" and pointing to the right. The well graded path switchbacks through an area of large trees, ferns and mossy rocks. The first significant feature is a log bridge crossing a small, rushing creek. Recently fitted with wire-mesh foot pads and a single wooden rail, the span is

easy and secure. After the bridge, the trail switchbacks near the creek.

3. When you can no longer hear the creek, you know you are about a third of the way up the mountain. After many more switchbacks the trail makes a long traverse to the right over a relatively gentle slope. This is your indication that you are roughly halfway.

4. As the switchbacks head uphill again, the way is a little steeper in spots. You will pass some cliffy bluffs looming above, still in the shadow of trees. One side route takes you a few steps to a beautiful viewpoint by a huge boulder. This is a good turnaround spot if you find you have bitten off more than you can chew.

5. As the trail starts to emerge from the trees, you may have to do a little light scrambling over rocky outcroppings, and in dry weather you may find areas of loose dirt that require careful footing. Here you will get increasing slices of view toward the peaks on the opposite side of the pass the highway leads through. You may be particularly interested in noting the contours of King's Peak, the large pyramidal mountain a little to the left, with its minor peak, often called Queen's Peak (see Hike 29).

6. The real treat comes when you emerge suddenly onto the shores of an exquisite tarn, or mountain lake. The whole rounded top of the mountain past here is dotted with smaller pools and occasional clusters of small trees. You can choose to make this your destination of course, but if you wish to gain the high point, make your way along the narrow trail to the left of the tarn. Various trails wind over the

The log-bridge creek crossing has a good walking surface and a solid handrail (2)

A view of Volcano Peak from one of the first viewpoints as the trail begins to emerge from the heavy forest (4)

rounded crest of knolls, but the highest point, complete with transmitter tower, is unambiguous. If visibility is low because of clouds, you are probably best off not going beyond the first and largest tarn unless you have a compass or GPS. Finding your way back to the trail down could be tricky.

7. Return the way you came.

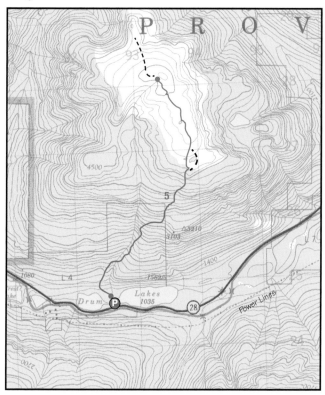

The view towards Puzzle Mountain and Mt. Colonel Foster (6)

28. Elk River to Landslide Lake

22 km return
High point: 905 m
Height gain: 680 m (cumulative)
Moderate / strenuous
May to October

Start: Taking Highway 28 from Campbell River toward Gold River, cross Buttle Lake and follow the Elk River valley until you see the BC Parks sign for the Elk River trailhead on the left.

Difficulty: Square orange tags with a diagonal stripe mark the way. The trail is generally very clear except at a few spots where small streams cross. All these have bridges, though, so you won't need to do any fording. The only slightly tricky part of the route is about 1 km before Landslide Lake. In wet weather it can be slippery crossing the smooth rock of a streambed scraped bare by the eponymous landslide. The same goes for climbing over a logjam just above this area. Those using the trail in winter or even spring need to be aware of the dangers of crossing snowy avalanche chutes.

Forested river valley with increasingly dramatic views of surrounding peaks and the devastating effects of a huge washout after the earthquake of 1946. Concludes with a stunning view of Landslide Lake and multi-peaked Mt. Colonel Foster, with one of the largest continuous cliff faces in the world.

1. Passing the outhouses, begin the wide, well graded trail as it ascends gradually through some magnificent old trees. The route crosses a strip of cleared land under power lines before switchbacking up and over a rise. A little beyond the end of the descent you will get your first view up Elk River itself.

2. The trail is largely level, through riverside forest, swinging away from the river for significant periods and traversing slopes well above it, occasionally passing giant boulders and some imposing ancient trees. Pass a beaver pond before coming to a sturdy bridge over Puzzle Creek, marked with a handmade wooden sign. A short distance later, come to a small stream which sometimes changes course and leaves a bridge spanning a dry creekbed. In most conditions, the stream is easily crossed.

3. Cross Volcano Creek (not signposted) with a view up toward a many-stepped falls. Descend past a bear cache line and an outhouse to gravel river flats and the first campsite a little more than halfway to the lake. This makes a suitable picnic spot and turnaround for those who would like a shortened version of the hike.

4. Cross another bridge. For the next section the trail crosses occasional avalanche chutes, streams and small waterfalls, during the summer largely comprising rocks and/or bare rock slab. Four-fifths of the way to the lake you will arrive at the second campsite, with an outhouse and several separate tent sites scattered amongst scrub trees on the gravel riverbank.

5. The rest of the trail to Landslide Lake passes through landscape much affected by the giant wave that swept down the riverbed after a chunk of Mt. Colonel Foster fell into the lake during the earthquake of 1946. Passing first through scrub trees, the path crosses the Elk River over a sturdy bridge and begins to ascend a little more steeply over bare rock marked with cairns.

6. The last phase of the route is indicated with a professionally painted sign saying "Landslide Lake 1 km" (though the segment seems much longer than that

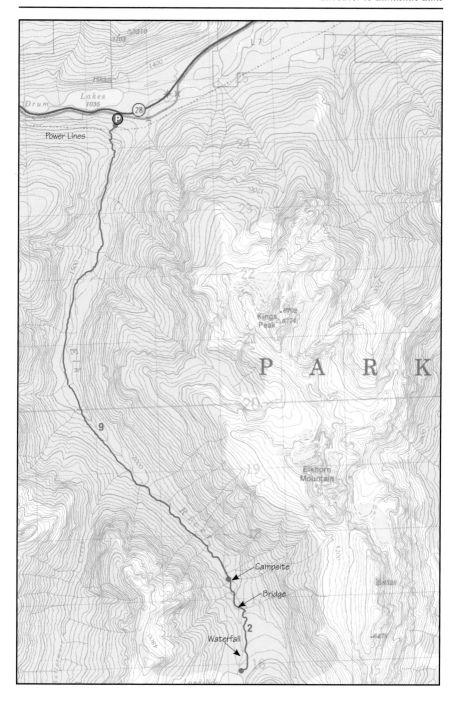

At many points the trail is significantly above the river, allowing views up the river valley (2)

because of the terrain and the 300 m of elevation gain). Entering the forest, the trail first switchbacks and then emerges again onto bare rock. From here you will have an excellent view of the many-stepped falls. Take care when crossing this section if the rock is wet. Even trickier in wet weather is a short section beyond this washout area where the trail traverses a small logjam. The final stretch to the lake over crests of bare rock dotted with scrub trees gives increasingly spectacular views of the crags of Mt. Colonel Foster and finally of the exposed chunk of mountain that gave the lake its name. The view of lake and peak has aptly been described as "one of the wonders of Vancouver Island."

7. Return the way you came.

Photograph by Christine Fordham. Mt. Colonel Foster and Landslide Lake (6)

The waterfall near the south end of the washout area and Landslide Lake (6)

29. King's Peak

15 km return
High point: 2065 m
Height gain: 1740 m
Very strenuous
Late June to October, depending
on snow cover

One of the two most challenging day hikes in this book. The eighth highest mountain on Vancouver Island and one of the most spectacular for its terrain and views of surrounding glaciers and peaks.

Difficulty: Well maintained and carefully engineered during the first part, the trail later deteriorates considerably. You will have to use your hands to grip roots on some steep (but not dangerous) sections. Later you will encounter unbridged (but quite easy) stream crossings, some scrambling along the dirt slope of a streamside gully and some careful (but unexposed) scrambling up a narrow rock gully. Start early to allow for a full day's trip.

Start: The trailhead is on Highway 28 between Campbell River and Gold River, about 8 km after you leave the western arm of Upper Campbell Lake. Before coming to the King's Peak sign, you will see a sign for the Elk River viewpoint. The trailhead is down a gravel road leading off the highway, signposted for King's Peak. However, you may wish to keep on past this sign if you would like a good view of the summit you are about to climb. A short distance along the road you will see a gravel pull-off and a labelled signpost pointing to the peak.

1. The first part of the trail is carefully engineered with board steps and switchbacks. At first you will gain little net elevation, since you rise over a crest and descend nearly as much. When you reach power lines, the route crosses a gravel track and heads into the forest. Here you will see another large trail sign. Crossing a stream via a little bridge, brace yourself for more seriously ascending terrain on a generally broad and clear track past some impressive firs.

2. The trail comes to the stream and more or less follows it for some distance.

The recommended route proceeds up the right bank to a waterfall before crossing. On stream crossings you will have to hop from rock to rock, but unless the water is particularly high this is usually not hard.

3. This section of trail up the left bank can be a little difficult, since you need to pick your way along eroded dirt sloping steeply toward the stream. Good boots help enormously. Use branches or roots for additional security if necessary. Usually this is the trickiest part of the whole route, but much depends on the degree of erosion from the previous winter and the number of hikers before you who have established a good track.

4. The trail crosses again to the right bank and ascends easily to an open, meadow-like area in a bowl surrounded by steep rock faces that rise impressively all around. Don't be tempted by the obvious direct route toward the peak up a narrow gully, or *couloir*. It is safe only for experienced climbers.

5. The route across this meadow, dotted with small trees and meandering streams, can be a little tricky because campers have created many cross trails. Look for orange flagging tape and head generally rightward to where the bowl narrows between cliffy areas. The way up this gully ascends steeply to The Ramparts and requires some use of hands.

6. You will emerge suddenly onto a ridge with splendid views across mountain peaks. This is a good turnaround place if you are running out of time or energy. Be

sure to notice what this spot looks like so you don't overshoot it on the return trip (though there is a route off the end of this ridge). Turn to the upward rocky slope. Look for cairns and ribbon when the path fades over solid rock. Again you may have to use your hands before the trail levels out and curves left.

7. When you get to the gap between the two peaks, you can make a detour to the lower peak on your left, but the main route carries on straight ahead to King's Peak. This lower peak you may see referred to (inaccurately) as "Queen's Peak" or "Queen's Face."

8. Follow cairns over the bumps to the summit, noting that you won't want to shortcut on your return trip, since there are cliffs to the north. From the summit you will have not only spectacular views of peaks in all directions, but also one of the most breathtaking views on the island: Mt. Elkhorn and its glacier look so close you will feel you can almost reach across to them.

9. Return the way you came.

Even when the creek is quite full crossing is not difficult (2)

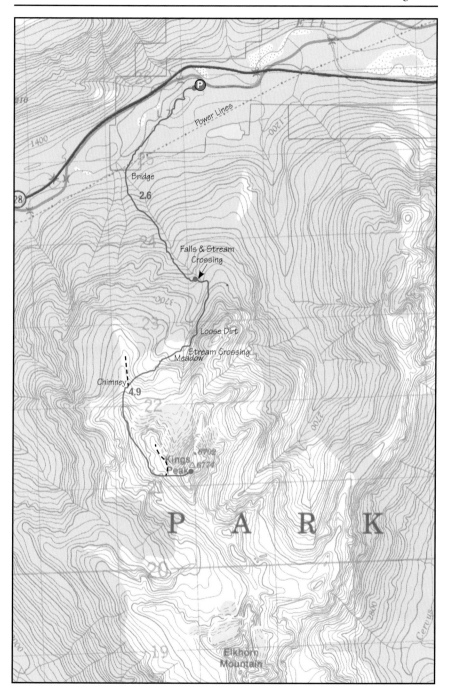

From the bowl of meadows and streams, a popular camping area, the route heads up a chimney-like chute at the low part of the ridge. Behind, so-called "Queen's Peak," a lower spur of King's Peak (4)

Mt. Elkhorn and its glacier viewed from the summit of King's Peak, through the haze of forest fire smoke drifting from BC's interior (8)

30. Augerpoint Mountain

11.5 km return
High point: 1839 m
Height gain: 1505 m
Strenuous
June to October

Switchbacks through forest to a gradual ascent along high, rocky table land studded with tiny tarns and great views of surrounding peaks and Buttle Lake.

Start: On Highway 28 between Campbell River and Gold River, turn down Western Mines Road just before the highway crosses the bridge over the narrows between Upper Campbell Lake and Buttle Lake. Set your trip odometer to zero, since the beginning of the trail is not signposted. Just before your odometer turns 20 km, slow down and creep along looking for a wider bit of shoulder for parking and a spray-painted arrow on the pavement. Its colour may vary between blue and orange and it may be faded, depending on the enthusiasm of volunteers. Usually there is also flagging tape at the narrow entrance to the path. If you miss it on your first pass, turn around at the Augerpoint Trail loop trail and come back 400 m.

Difficulty: This is not a publicly maintained park trail. It was built by a local, Jack Shark, to bypass a forest fire area and rejoin a former route. Though unsignposted, it is a clear trail and well used by, amongst others, private and commercially guided groups making the backpacking traverse from Paradise Meadows and Mt. Albert Edward. Hiking over loose gravel and tree roots will require some care. Climbing Augerpoint Mountain requires basic scrambling and care but no technical skill.

1. The trail, unlike the trailhead, is clear. The first part of it is steep, but only by hiking standards. You may have to climb over the occasional fallen tree, depending on the storms of the previous winter. You will be rewarded with a good viewpoint over Buttle Lake and a rest stop in this forested section. After several switchbacks the trail approaches a pond. At this point the way levels out somewhat, dipping slightly southeast before once again starting to climb. After several more switchbacks the trees begin to thin out.

2. As the trail emerges into increasingly open areas, it starts to traverse southeast, parallel to the lake and ridge, at first below the high part of the ridge. During the first part of this traverse you will pass some particularly attractive ponds before crossing two streams. Normally, neither stream poses any difficulties, though this area can retain snow into the summer.

3. The route reaches the top of the ridge (1586 m) and stays high, more or less, for the rest of the hike. Depending on the time of year, you may have to cross some snowfields as well as sections of scree and outcroppings of solid rock. The broad ridge drops slightly from your first high point, giving some good views of Shark Lake on your left.

4. Climb gradually from the first high point, curving from southeast to northeast along the ridgeline. Another high point, at 1730 m, makes a satisfying turnaround or rest spot. Good views here of Ruth Masters Lake. Syd Watts Peak is the name of the close high point to the south, which too is a feasible destination. Mt. Albert Edward, the highest peak in the immediate area, towers above Augerpoint Mountain.

5. Return the way you came.

Option:

If you have the time and inclination, you can continue to Augerpoint Mountain. This requires a little scrambling but no technical ability. This is about a 2 km return trip, involving a cumulative gain of a little over 200 vertical metres on the outbound trip and 100 on the return. Scramble down to the obvious ridge to the northeast, losing about 100 m of elevation, before scrambling up along the continuation of this ridge to reach Augerpoint itself, at 1839 m.

Shark Lake can be reached by a scramble from the low part of the ridge. Even in mid summer it can trap lingering snow (4)

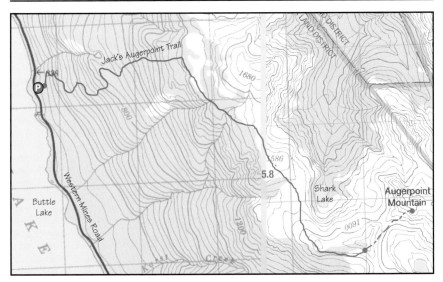

The view back along the ridge and across Buttle Lake. The trail from the lake reaches the ridge near its low point (4)

131

Looking beyond the southwest end of Buttle Lake to Mt. Myra. A superbly scenic but challenging day hike can be made to Mt. Myra

Mt. Jutland and Mt. Albert Edward viewed from a high point near Augerpoint Mountain at the end of a hot, dry summer

31. Flower Ridge

15 km return (many options)
High point: 1470 m
Height gain: 1195 m
Strenuous
June to October

*Forests and striking views
down Buttle Lake. Subalpine
ridge with beautiful little tarns,
clusters of trees and 360-degree
views of glaciers and peaks.*

Start: Take Highway 28 from Campbell River toward Gold River. At the sharp turn to head across Buttle Lake, carry on straight ahead along Western Mines Road until you see the BC Parks sign for Flower Ridge.

Difficulty: The trail itself is well graded, but with this much ascent, of course, it can be strenuous if taken too quickly. Still, it is generally less steep than similar trails in the park. The only difficulties come with fallen trees if the parks crew has not cleared them.

1. The trailhead is clearly signposted and accompanied by a sister sign warning you that you should carry your own water. The first part of the trail climbs only gradually under an open and airy canopy of fir and hemlock. For some distance the route roughly follows the course of a stream, mostly in a ravine to the left of the trail.

2. The path swings away from the stream, occasionally passing large mossy rocks and climbing over some rough sections of root. When you reach a rounded bluff, take the time to leave the trail and enjoy the spacious views of Mt. Myra, Phillips Ridge, the south end of Buttle Lake and, less scenically, the Westmin mineworks at the base of Phillips Ridge

3. The trail continues a little more steeply at points. Depending on how much damage has been done by snow during the winter and how much clearing has been done by parks workers, you may have to climb over fallen trees. As the standing trees become noticeably shorter and more widely spaced, the trail occasionally climbs over bald rock.

4. Once you have come to an increasingly open ridge area with ponds and

The view north along the heavily glaciated peaks above Buttle Lake (4)

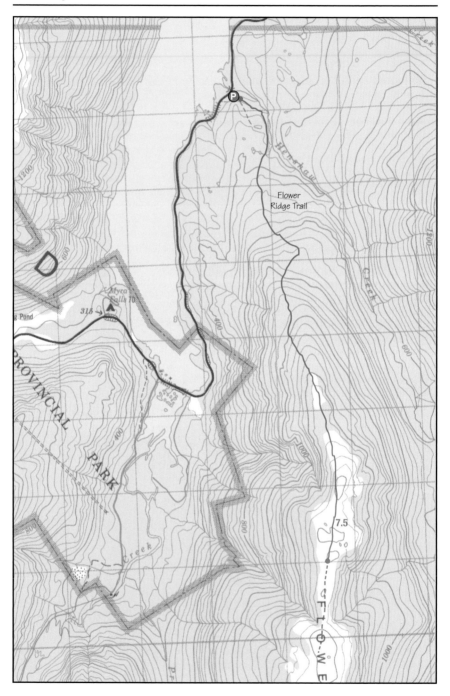

distant views, you can choose just about anywhere as your rest and turnaround spot. Those who want a strong sense of destination should follow the trail over stretches of bare rock (with small cairns), possibly over patches of lingering snow, to the high section of ridge that is just over 1400 m (depending which bump you choose) and about 6 km from the trailhead.

Option:

If you are ambitious and enjoy ridgewalking, you can go an additional 3 or 4 km along the rising and falling ridge, over lingering snowfields and past more tarns while gaining only an additional 20 or 30 m of elevation. (Backpackers use this trail to get to many different backcountry routes, some of them quite difficult. Don't expect the path to come to an abrupt halt anywhere.)

Mt. Myra rises from the east shore of Buttle Lake

32. Bedwell Lake

12 km return
High point: 953 m
Height gain: 450 m
Moderately strenuous
June to October

Deep forest, river crossings, a carefully engineered trail with ladders and steps. A beautiful wilderness lake surrounded by mountains.

Start: Take Highway 23 from Campbell River toward Gold River, but when the road turns right to cross the bridge over the narrows between Upper Campbell Lake and Buttle Lake, continue straight ahead on Western Mines Road. Past the south end of Buttle Lake, turn left onto a gravel road signposted for Bedwell Lake. At a fork, also signposted for Bedwell Lake, continue left. The first part of this road is the roughest. If your vehicle makes it comfortably past this, you should have no difficulty driving the rest of the way. After 7 km and a considerable climb, you will reach the parking area and posted signs for Bedwell Lake trailhead, 200 m from the parking area.

Difficulty: Since an enormous amount of work has gone into improving this much used and heavily eroded trail, there are few difficulties. Still, because of continuing erosion, some parts of the route have loose, unstable rocks. Otherwise, as long as hikers are comfortable with ladders and sometimes slippery wood, the difficulties are minimal. Although elevations are comparatively low, this area is quick to attract snow in the fall and slow to let go of it in the spring.

1. Passing the outhouse and posted map, walk 200 m along the gravel road. Turn left into the forest and onto a broad, gradually descending, zigzagging trail, passing some imposing root masses of fallen trees. You will soon cross a suspension bridge over a rocky channel, then a wooden bridge over Thelwood Creek.

2. The impressively engineered trail switchbacks steeply through some majestic rocks and rock faces away from

and above the creek before rejoining it. A second set of switchbacks is much gentler and smoother. After levelling a little you come to a third set of switchbacks, this time through a maze of giant boulders.

3. After a fairly flat section with the creek in a deep gorge to your right, the trail descends a little to the creek. Several bridges in rapid succession take you to the opposite bank. From here to Baby Bedwell Lake the path is often quite rooty and steep, but it is clear and well outfitted with steps, boardwalks and metal ladders at the steepest parts. The route rises and drops through some small meadows with ponds in a kind of cleft just before this smaller Baby Bedwell Lake. The best views are from the camping area a short distance along the trail to the right.

4. The through route swings around the lakeshore, then steeply ascends a rocky bluff separating Baby Bedwell from Bedwell (the two lakes you see on this route are, however, at nearly the same elevation). Several more sets of metal stairs lead to a wonderful vantage point on the lakes, the surrounding mountains and some tiny rocky islets. This makes a good turnaround spot if you are short on time or energy.

5. The trail descends steeply via the most vertiginous of the several ladder sequences to the shore of Bedwell Lake and beautiful views of the islets and peaks. After following the shore nearly to the south end of the lake, the track leads into some forest with surprisingly large trees. There are three fairly easy stream crossings and you will see the remnants of

small, washed-out bridges. At the camping area there is good swimming (the lake becomes reasonably warm), an outhouse and attractive bluffs from which to drink in the view.

6. Return the way you came.

The beginning of the giant boulder maze of switchbacks (2)

Option:

The popular trail to Bedwell Lake is often used as an entry to extended backpacking trips. You may wish to follow the signposted track to gain a little elevation and some good views (the alternative trail, to Bedwell Sound, is currently closed). Be aware, however, that you would need proper equipment before going much beyond the lake.

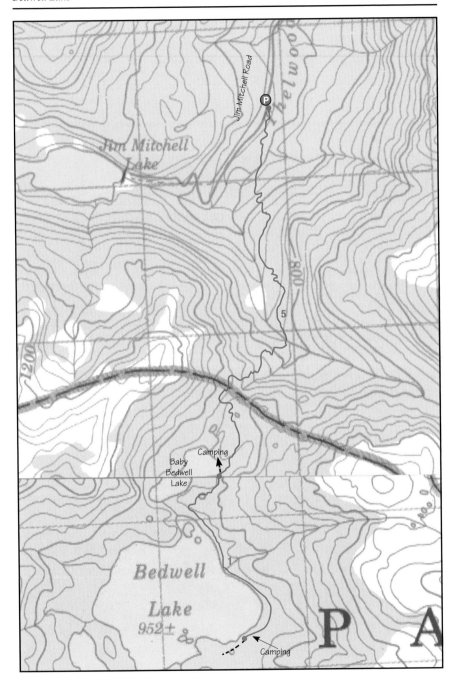

Looking along the shore of Bedwell Lake to the camping area at the south end and Big Interior Mountain (5)

33. *Mount Myra*

17 km return
High Point: 1814 m
Height gain: 1425 m
Very strenuous
Late June to October depending on
snow cover

Lakes and garden-like subalpine vegetation followed by a long, curving ridge to the peak and views of the main Strathcona peaks, glaciers and Buttle Lake.

Start: From Campbell River, take Highway 23 toward Gold River. After 48 km, where the highway swings right to cross between the lakes, carry on straight ahead on Western Mines Road to the Westmin Mine. Mt. Myra is the pyramidal peak looming over the end of the lake, though the hiking route approaches from the back. Parking can be a little confusing, though the Provincial Parks sign for Tennant Lake is clearly visible by the side of the road as you near the end of the mining works and the asphalt road heads uphill. To the left you will see a gated gravel road and to the right a gravel parking area beside some mill buildings. Park here and walk across the paved road, down the gravel road and past the gate.

Difficulty: Loose, jagged gravel and rock on the washed-out roadbed during the approach can be hard on ankles. The route up gullies requires hands, sometimes making use of bush branches, but there are no exposed drops. Once on the ridge, make sure you spot the next cairn or occasional piece of flagging tape to keep on the trail, especially because after a winter of heavy snow, patches can linger well into August or even September. In addition, dry streambeds can sometimes look like a trail. Some climb the mountain year round because of relatively low avalanche danger. Such trips require proper equipment and training.

1. You will pass the trailheads to Phillips Ridge and Upper Myra Falls as you walk along this gravel road. Cross a road bridge over a beautiful rushing river beside buildings associated with a small power-plant. After the bridge, and after several kilometres along a gravel bulldozer track, begin the ascent to Tennant Lake. The steep track has eroded to rough boulders, though ferns and other attractive vegetation are increasingly making this route more like a trail. The first part of the road passes magnificent old-growth trees, but these thin out as you ascend.

2. About halfway up this part of the ascent you will have to cross fast-flowing Tennant Creek over a narrow footbridge positioned beside the large pipe that carries water from the lake. A single rope handrail makes the crossing a little less dizzying and the footing is secure. The trail/road changes character after you cross the creek since it climbs steeply in a kind of gully and the vegetation begins to look somewhat subalpine. You will need to cross another (small) stream over huge cubic stepping stones.

3. The road ends at the foot of a boulder-faced dam about 8 m high. Find your way diagonally across these boulders to the left. Once on the level of the lake, walk over the narrow concrete rims of two small dams. You will have to pull yourself up a short, steep lip to get onto the first of a sequence of granite ridges interspersed with pools. This whole section is a striking natural rock garden.

4. At the end of the "rock garden," the trail goes through its least pleasant section, requiring you to squeeze between small evergreens, clamber over a few big boulders and scramble up some fairly

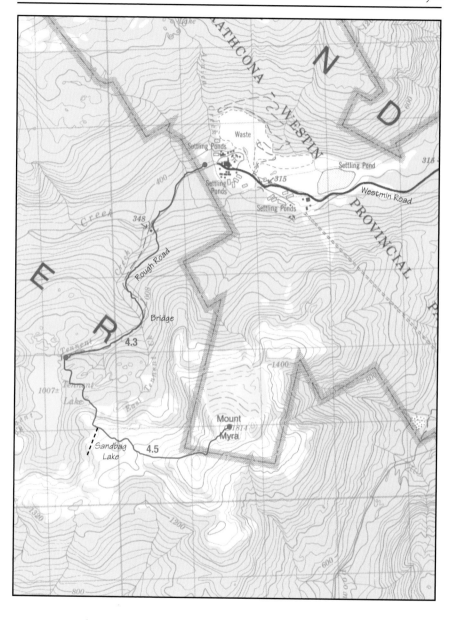

steep rock sections. Once you are on the ridge, the trail largely follows the high points of the rocky bumps along the ridge as it makes a large curve to the left (east). Shortly after reaching the ridge you will come across a junction. Go left to keep high on the ridge.

5. You will pass a beautiful small lake, unofficially called Sandbag Lake (a good turnaround spot if you are getting tired). Follow the cairns along the broad ridge, avoiding the temptation to shortcut across the curving route. The trail splits before a false summit, but both routes work and rejoin at the high point.

6. Drop down a little into a saddle/col

before beginning the final section. The main route goes straight up a bushy gully, where again you will have to use your hands. You may feel a little exposed here, so do take care. At the top of this gully follow the cairns to the left to reach the summit.

7. From the large cairn at the summit, appreciate the 360 degree views. You may be particularly interested in picking out Augerpoint to the northeast and Flower Ridge to the southeast (Hikes 30 and 31). To the southwest you may be able identify, in sequence, Mt. Septimus, Mt. Rousseau, Big Interior Mountain and Mt. Tom Taylor.

8. Return the way you came.

Looking west from a section of trail along the high ridge near the summit

Opposite top: The crystal clear water of East Tennant Creek viewed from the bridge on the approach road

Opposite bottom: Tennant Lake marks the end of the old service road, and the beginning of the trail

34. Canyon View / Elk Falls

10.8 km loop
High point: 170 m
Height gain: 150 m
Easy / moderate
All season

Riverside trails, a high canyon bridge, old-growth giants and a spectacular waterfall.

Start: From Highway 19 passing by the northwest end of Campbell River, turn left onto Highway 28 to Gold River. Some 1.5 km along, turn in to the parking lot located on the right-hand side next to a large sign for Elk Falls Provincial Park.

Difficulty: Except for one short user-made section with a few roots and occasional mud patches, all the trails are broad, well graded and surfaced with crushed gravel. Bridges, boardwalks and stairs are provided at steep places, and guardrails are in place at dangerous spots.

Several combinations of routes are possible, but by following the recommended one, you visit the most spectacular and remote points in the middle of your walk.

1. Begin by having a look at the information signs about salmon fishing in the Campbell River. Start downriver by turning right and almost immediately cross a small bridge along Highway 28. Once across the bridge find the first of several small fisherman-made dirt trails down to and along the bank.

2. Cross the river on the road bridge and turn left to the signposted "Canyon View Trail." This part of the track runs through large spruce and hemlock immediately next to a small spawning channel. When you come to a pumphouse, bypass it along gravel roads to return to the riverside trail. This section runs close to the bank of the wide, rushing river. Toward its northwest end the route climbs, drops and again climbs high via some stairs to reach the top of the canyon.

3. Cross the sturdy little footbridge over the spectacular gorge with excellent views of the curving river. After following the trail toward the hydroelectric plant on the southwest bank, turn right onto the broad gravel path signposted to Elk Falls. The first section of this connector route, leading to the falls, is the "Millennium Trail." The Millennium climbs via some switchbacks and elevated walkways through fairly mature second-growth forest. At one section the suspended walkway crosses an impressive little gorge full of devil's club. Also watch for the large, hollow cedar with an interesting "doorway." After climbing, the trail levels out before descending to reach Elk Falls Provincial Park. Close to the park you will pass some gigantic Douglas firs and cedars.

4. Cross the parking lot and follow the only trail a short distance until, at a T-junction, you see a sign pointing to the right toward a viewpoint. Follow this track, passing some magnificent old-growth trees, down to a stretch of exposed riverbed immediately above the thundering falls. Explore this area, taking care not to slip in wet weather or venture too close to the falls. Return to the trail to go to the viewing platform over the 25 m high falls. Although you will be viewing the cataract from an angle, the configuration of cliffs, deep gorge and huge cascade is spectacular.

5. Return to the T-junction, but instead of climbing back up the trail you came down, continue straight ahead. This route runs fairly close to the river, past a sequence of narrow channels and broad pools until you get to a viewpoint looking toward a rush of water. The trail zigzags up a high

bank to pass a second parking lot and, via a feeder trail, returns to the first parking lot and the trailhead for the Millennium Trail.

6. Return along the Millennium. When you come to a signposted fork near the canyon bridge and the power station, go slightly right to keep straight ahead down the fairly steep trail. Crossing over the river directly in front of the roaring turbines, past chain-link fences and metal staircases, can be a little intimidating. Perhaps contrary to your first impressions, this route is open to the public.

7. Follow the path a short distance to a large parking lot (with facilities) and, via a short set of stairs, pick up Canyon View Trail. Much of this route, through spruce and alder, runs alongside a spawning channel rather than the main river, but is nevertheless beautiful and shaded. Trying to ignore the increasingly close whoosh of traffic along the nearby road, return to your starting point.

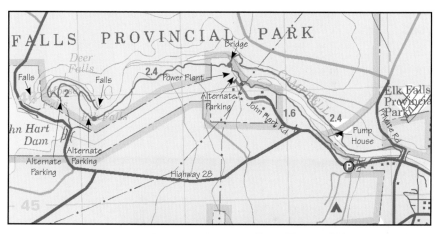

Below the hydro station the fast-flowing Elk River is a prime spot for fishermen (1)

Opposite: The Millennium Trail towards Elk Falls Park has some picturesque "character" trees (3)

Elk Falls drops into a narrow gorge with impressive cliffs angling across the viewing platform (4)

35. Ripple Rock

8.2 km return
High point: 95 m
Height gain: ~270 m (cumulative)
Easy / moderate
All season but can be muddy

Start: Drive north of Campbell River along Highway 19. About 10 km along you will pass a large pulp mill. The trailhead is 2.4 km after this, at a gravel parking lot that is hard to spot, situated below the highway and to the right. Before this parking lot you will see a sign indicating the turnoff to be in 400 m, but the distance seems much less.

Difficulty: The trail has been recently upgraded with many improvements, principally a suspension bridge and a large staircase. The path requires some careful footing on rocky and rooty sections but there is no exposure or danger.

Lots of variety in terrain, views and geographical features en route to a spectacular, clifftop viewpoint over the surging tidal whirlpools of Seymour Narrows. This was the site of one of the world's largest non-nuclear peacetime explosions, set off in 1958 to remove the notorious Ripple Rock, which had been responsible for many shipwrecks and 114 deaths.

1. The first part of the trail is the least inspiring but nevertheless is a pleasant, gradual descent through salmonberry bushes. Sections of board and gravel steps give the option of avoiding the sometimes muddy path to the side. Crossing the new suspension bridge over Menzies Creek is a bit of a carnival adventure in keeping

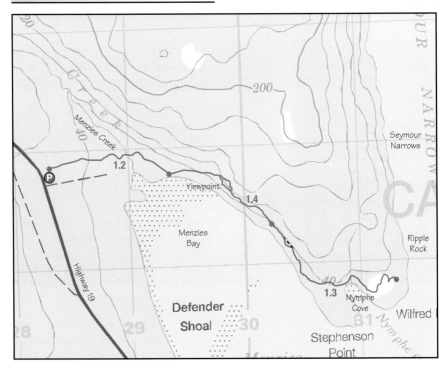

Beds of pink fawn lilies in the low ground near the head of Menzies Bay (1)

your balance. A huge Sitka spruce at the end of the bridge is the impressive anchor. A level, bushy section of path soon brings you to the tidal flats of Menzies Bay, with a signposted viewpoint.

2. The trail passes over a boardwalk and begins a gradual traversing climb through a beautiful forest of mossy rocks, firs and swordferns. When you cross a small wooden bridge, look for the remains of a historical skidway that was used for dragging logs into the bay. When you come across two signs, one indicating the main trail, the other a viewpoint, take the right fork to the viewpoint. This bluff of mossy rock (and, in May, of camas lilies) has beautiful views over Menzies Bay and the peaks of Strathcona Provincial Park. You need not retrace your route to get to the main trail, since a small path carries on past the view to get back to the main track.

3. Rejoining the main trail, go a short distance before climbing a short set of stairs, then passing a picnic table and later a log bench. When you get to a fork with a sign pointing to the right, take that option, though you will find yourself dropping down through a small gully before reascending to join the old trail. The old (higher) trail cuts across a rocky area and is a little narrow in spots but currently usable. Once it crosses Enson Point, the path drops to the upper shore of Nymphe Cove, a pleasant rest or picnic spot.

4. Climb up a section of rock that can be slick when wet. Continue upward until you come to an impressive set of stairs giving you quick and easy access to the top of the ridge at Wilfred Point. Before climbing the stairs, however, follow the "Viewpoint" sign a short way to an open, mossy area with a picnic table

This surprisingly bouncing and swaying suspension bridge is anchored to a huge spruce (1)

and magnificent views of the peaks of Strathcona Park: from left to right, Mt. Albert Edward, jagged Mt. Elkhorn and, to its north, King's Peak.

5. It is only a short distance from the top of the staircase across the ridge to the cliffs overlooking Seymour Narrows and, directly opposite, tiny Maud Island and massive Quadra Island. If you arrive here during maximum current, you will be treated to the spectacle of powerful whirlpools, upwellings and standing waves as huge volumes of ocean water try to surge past this bottleneck into and out of the Strait of Georgia. The remains of the infamous Ripple Rock lie beneath the surface almost immediately below the viewpoint and about a third of the way across the channel. A giant cruise ship or freighter squeezing down this passage is likewise an impressive sight.

6. Return the same way you came.

Menzies Bay at low tide (1)

Looking north across Seymour Narrows and a low point on Quadra Island (5)

Useful Contacts

BC Parks
www.env.gov.bc.ca/bcparks

Capital Regional District Parks
Parks & Environmental Services
490 Atkins Avenue
Victoria, BC V9B 2Z8
tel: 250.478.3344
fax: 250.478.5416
www.crd.bc.ca/parks

Cowichan Valley Regional District
175 Ingram St
Duncan, BC V9L 1N8

250.746.2500
1.800.665.3955
www.cvrd.bc.ca

Regional District of Nanaimo
Recreation & Parks Services
Oceanside Place
830 W Island Hwy
Parksville, BC V9P 2X4
tel: 250.248.3252
toll free within BC: 1.888.828.2069
fax: 250.248.3159
recparks@rdn.bc.ca
www.rdn.bc.ca

Acknowledgements

Thanks to those who tromped these trails with me and provided advice and information, hiking companionship, photographs and/or GPS tracks: Eileen Dombrowski, Megan Dombrowski, Catrin Brown, Arno Dirks, Bill Thompson, Aldous Sperl, David Pinel, Harry Indrickson, Tim Allix, Christine Fordham and Mike Watson.